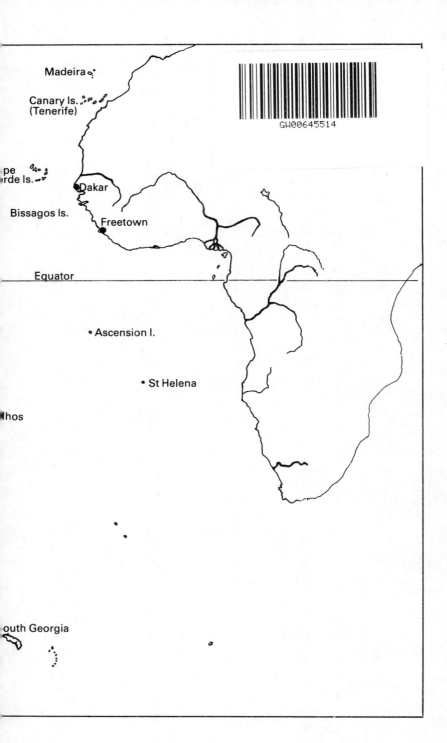

Madeira

Canary Is.
(Tenerife)

pe
rde Is.

Bissagos Is.

Dakar

Freetown

Equator

• Ascension I.

• St Helena

hos

outh Georgia

THE ENEMY FOUGHT SPLENDIDLY

THE ENEMY FOUGHT SPLENDIDLY

Being the 1914~1915 diary of the Battle of the Falklands & its aftermath by Surgeon T.B. Dixon R.N.V.R. of H.M.S. Kent

BLANDFORD PRESS
POOLE · DORSET

First published in the U.K. 1983 by
Blandford Press, Link House, West Street,
Poole, Dorset, BH15 1LL

Distributed in the United States by
Sterling Publishing Co., Inc., 2 Park
Avenue, New York, N.Y. 10016.

British Library Cataloguing in Publication Data

Dixon, T. B.
　The enemy fought splendidly.
　1. World War 1914-1918 – Naval operations, British
　– Personal narratives
　I. Title
　940.4'54　　　　　　　D582.F2

ISBN 0 7137 1326 7

Typeset in 11/12½pt Garamond by August Filmsetting, Warrington, Cheshire

Printed and bound in Great Britain by Biddles Ltd, Guildford and King's Lynn

CONTENTS

Editorial Note		vi
Foreword		vii
Introduction		ix
1	Before the Battle	1
2	Battles of the Falklands	26
3	Search and Chase	32
4	Sinking the *Dresden*	58
5	Aftermath	63

Appendix I: *South Atlantic Naval Battle;
   Bristol Doctor's Graphic Account*   78

Appendix II: *Naval List for H.M.S. Kent 1914, 1915
   and 1916*   81

Appendix III: *Illustrated list of British Ships involved
   in the Battle of the Falklands*   85

Bibliography   91

Biographical Note   91

Index   92

EDITORIAL NOTE

Except for a few missing sketches this book is complete and unabridged. Editorial policy has been to introduce paragraphs, to standardise spelling – while retaining Dixon's idiosyncrasies – to restrict the use of capital letters and to explain or expand abbreviations.

FOREWORD

Some fifteen or so years after this log was written, David Falkland
Dixon and I were in the same house at Clifton College and Dr T. B.
Dixon was my family's doctor. He was also a Surgeon Captain
R.N.V.R. attached to H.M.S. *Flying Fox*, headquarters of the
Severn Division of the Volunteer Reserve. Already, at the age of
fourteen, I was keenly interested in the Navy but his many
invitations to that ship helped to crystallise my determination to
enter the Service.

When I joined H.M.S. *Frobisher* in 1933 as a Cadet, attitudes and
conditions in the Navy had changed remarkably little from those
described in this book. The gun, and in particular the big gun, still
dominated Naval thinking. Six-inch gun cruisers, which were not
all that dissimilar from H.M.S. *Kent*, were still going down the
slipways, and tactics were designed to bring such guns and those of
the great battleships to bear on the enemy.

Admittedly, aircraft carriers had taken their place in the fleet,
but inadequate priority was afforded to this arm of the Service and
naval aircraft were obsolescent. It took the World War 2 battles in
the Pacific to bring into sharp focus the devastating potential of air
power to attack ships at sea or in harbour, and to change the
concept of naval warfare. Recent actions during the Falklands
Crisis, in the same geographical area of operations as those
described in this log have served to demonstrate once again the
vulnerability of surface ships to air attack and the need for some
measure of at least local air superiority.

The conditions under which the sailors lived had little changed.

There was perhaps a little more space but broadside messes, totally lacking in any privacy or comfort, were still the fashion. The system of feeding by a kind of self-catering by messes provided a dull if filling diet. Not until after World War 2 did the conditions on the lower deck start to improve and the wide gap in the standards of living between officers and ratings begin to narrow.

In such conditions, H.M.S. *Kent* went to war in 1914 with Surgeon Dixon among her company. This book describes his daily life over the early part of a commission which was to last for three years overseas. (Nowadays, nine months is considered to be the maximum separation of men from their families tolerable in peacetime.) It emphasises the boredom, frustration and often great discomfort of wartime patrols; the days, weeks and even months of steaming without a decent 'run ashore', and the ever-present and unpleasant prospect of frequent coaling. What a difference a helicopter would have made to all that searching: nowadays one is carried on the quarter deck as standard practice.

For the surgeon himself, little provision was made. He had to make do with improvised facilities in any space where he would not be in the way. It is remarkable how uncomplaining and tolerant that branch of the Service was with their lot in action.

But if war in the *Kent* was for the most part boring, there were moments of intense excitement. Ships sighted, chased and boarded. And, of course, the Battle of the Falklands and the chase of the *Dresden*, both of which are vividly described. Dancing, by the officers on the quarter-deck during the latter chase, with the enemy in sight but out of range, is hard to imagine!

I am sure this log will be enjoyed by all those interested in Naval life of that period and there is in it much of interest to fishermen and ornithologists as well.

Admiral Sir John Bush
Hampshire, 4 July 1982

INTRODUCTION

This is my Grandfather's diary, kept over the first part of a voyage, in H.M.S. *Kent*, which lasted for over two years during World War 1. When I first started to decipher it from his doctor's handwriting (which deteriorated in proportion to the vibration of the ship's engines), I had only the vaguest memories of him, and only a knowledge of the history from family legends. As I went through the diary I realised that it was of more than a purely personal interest. He wrote about life on board, the trips ashore, the scenery and wildlife, the historic actions and the human detail with such a breadth of observation and humour that one is drawn into the narrative and further to a liking for the writer himself.

The recent revival of interest in the Falkland Islands makes the account in this diary, and in the Bristol paper (Appendix I), of the original battle in 1914 particularly fascinating.

Britain had been badly defeated at the Battle of Coronel several weeks before and the Battle of the Falklands was her fortunate comeback. For those who care to pursue more of the history, a short Bibliography is provided (the parallels and connections of this action with the Battle of the River Plate in World War 2 are also worth studying).

The one German ship which escaped after the Battle of the Falklands, the *Dresden*, became the focus for the next part of the diary. The *Dresden* disappeared and the *Kent* was sent in search of her, thus starting an anxious game of hide and seek along the intricate coastline of South America, which lasted for months.

The news that my Grandmother, Norah, had borne them a son

appears in the last part of the diary. At one stage in her pregnancy she thought herself widowed, because when the *Kent* lost wireless contact during the battle and a thick fog came on delaying their return to Port Stanley, news reached Britain that the *Kent* was thought to have been sunk. In fact, the wireless house had been destroyed but not the whole ship, and my Grandfather was alive and well. In celebration of this their son was christened Falkland.

This son was my Father. He first saw his own father at the age of two, and his initial reaction (see page 77) could not have been more strongly reversed in later life. He greatly admired his father, and the same is true for me. It was my father who encouraged and helped me with this diary's publication, and I would like it to be a tribute to both my Father and Grandfather.

I would like to thank Admiral Sir John Bush for contributing the Foreword, and Dr Mary Dixon and Miss Annabelle Dixon (daughter and granddaughter of the author respectively) for their help with the illustrations. I would also like to acknowledge Stuart Booth, Jonathan Grimwood and others of Blandford Press for enabling it to be published.

Rose Dixon
Dagnall, December 1982

BEFORE THE BATTLE

Monday October 12th 1914. Off at last after a week of hanging round Portsmouth with steam trials, engine defects and coaling. The weather inclined to break up, but quite smooth as we steam along past the Needles. Have just been informed by the Captain of Marines (Laing) that we are making for St Vincent, Cape Verde Islands. Have just snapped the *Europa* as she returns to harbour. Her queer striped funnels have been our chief view for 10 days.

6 p.m. Beginning to roll. Can't face dinner and so to bed.

Tuesday October 13th. In the Bay. Got up and shaved this morning after a good vomit, but had to return to bunk with breakfast. Stayed there dressed most of the day, vomiting at intervals, but fairly cheerful between whiles. Can't keep a thing down, not even water. My great comfort to suck an apple, of which I have a store of Cox's Orange Pippin.

This afternoon the Principal Medical Officer (P.M.O.), Fleet Surgeon Pickthorn, came down hurriedly to say we were chasing a tramp steamer which refused to give any account of herself. Made a great effort and got up on deck. Great excitement as we overhauled her and got her at last on our starboard beam, whereupon she ran up strings of flags and proved herself a British collier. The sea running huge and every promise of a dirty night. Got into bunk at last again. Fairly comfy after vomit and able to analyse the different sounds. Ship rolling terribly. Glass and china being smashed all round. Bookcases and piano in wardroom all over the place. Paymaster was trying to play the piano when it rushed at him and pinned him up against the table. Hear also that the Padre nearly lost, walking calmly about the quarter-deck with big seas coming over! Rescued in time by Lieutenant Redhead. Must keep Padre. He plays piano too well to lose. Very sick. Very rough night. Most officers feeling sick too, I hear. P.M.O. most kind all day, looking in and cheering me up and doing little jobs. Couldn't be nicer. Surgeon Burn ill too.

Wednesday October 14th. Very rough night of it. Kept waking up and listening to terrible noises of breaking. Told that we nearly lost a boat in the night. Mess deck awash and the ship's crew very sick. Feeling better and kept down a cup of tea and biscuit.

Got up midday and ventured on deck. Bright sun, much warmer and sea rolling across our beam in huge waves. Retired to bunk for lunch of Bovril and biscuit. After sleep came on deck and after tea walked the quarter-deck for two hours. Very pleased with myself at quick recovery, albeit legs a little shaky. Had quite a good dinner with the mess, too. Off the coast of Spain somewhere. Mother Carey's chickens and two dolphins seen. Much warmer.

Thursday October 15th. A most interesting day. Towards noon picked up smoke of a steamer and gave chase. Steamer altered course and behaved as if she had lost her wits. Our guns trained on her and she finally came on our starboard and stopped. Much flag wagging on both sides. She turned out to be the *Oetz*, Danish craft from Bahia to Gibraltar. The boat had meanwhile been got ready to take the Prize Lieutenant aboard and her crew were waiting to lower away. However, this wasn't necessary. The Dane asked us to tell her where she was exactly and we separated, she running up a polite thank-you in gaudy flags.

I slept after lunch and after tea the officers started games on the quarter-deck. A vaulting horse was procured and the snotties[1] made to exercise thereon by the instructor. Some of us joined in later; hockey with corks for balls. A weird game, but exciting. After that leapfrog and then follow-my-leader. I soon had enough. Am still keeping up the fiction of being an invalid, though don't feel like one. Boxing between the snotties most uneasy to watch.

[1] Naval slang for Midshipmen.

One novice particularly fierce and ineffective. The P.M.O. and I walked on deck till dinner and watched the contest. The sea much calmer and a deep blue today while it's been quite warm even on the bridge at night.

After dinner, dramatic chase of another steamer. P.M.O. sighted lights on the port bow. Two minutes later ship's course altered and we gave chase. The whole ship woken up and sent to General Quarters. This for the medical staff means the bowels of the ship. I went down there and the temperature next to the boiler being unbearable, had to come up for air. Found myself, after climbing many ladders, up on the fo'c'sle just under the conning tower. Could hear the Captain inside, shouting down the tubes to all parts of the ship and giving directions to the gun crews in the turrets.

All our lights are darkened at night and this stealthy rush through the gloom very exciting. Suddenly a fizzle above on the bridge and our searchlights are playing on a huge tramp steamer half a mile away. She proves to be English bound for South America and we pass on. We must have considerably startled her. A balmy night, the Padre playing in the Mess and the Paymaster and I keeping watch outside the wireless room ready to decode any message coming through. The war very far away seemingly.

Friday October 16th. A rather tame morning. Increasing heat and a general feeling of lassitude and disinclination to work. This afternoon we made a target out of planks and some red bunting and having heaved it overboard practised gunnery with 3 pounder insets in the 6-inch guns at 2–3,000 yards. Noise not so bad as the bark: vicious bark of the 3 pounder is silenced inside the 6-inch gun. Results good. Fore turret (Lilley's) sights evidently wrong. Finally rammed the target in picking it up and did more damage to it than by all the firing of the 240 rounds! Starboard guns only used.

The heat in the wardroom in the evening most uncomfortable, but very nice on deck after. The wake; one glitter of phosphorescent particles. Venus so bright that its line of reflection equalled that of the moon on the water in England.

P.S. Quite forgot that at 6 a.m. we sighted Madeira on our port bow. The sunrise behind the 6,000 ft peaks of the island most impressive, but owing to the direction of the sun couldn't make out much of the details of the island. Wished very badly we could have explored the place.

Saturday October 17th. Quite hot 7 a.m. Sea dead calm and fine cumulus cloud effects Africa way. As the day wore on the increasing heat made us long for whites which are to be worn tomorrow. Feeling very limp. Before lunch started on censorship duties with P.M.O. in his cabin. Most of the cards and letters pathetically brief owing to instruction. Dozens of husbands writing less than 18 words all told to their wives.

After tea, climbed into the foretop with Danckwerts to view the fire-control methods up there. Found the climb unexpectedly trying owing to the motion of the ship, giddiness and lack of condition of my muscles, possibly owing to big dose of Eno's this morning. However, stuck to it and was rewarded by a fine view of the whole ship and a cool breeze. Gunnery test rather a fiasco owing to the failure of the dynamo supplying current to the telephones and guns. Only a few rounds fired therefore. Took one photo from the foretop loking down on deck. The toast in the mess tonight *'sweethearts and wives'*. The Padre dines with the Skipper.

Sunday October 18th. Everyone turned up at breakfast in whites. All the seats have white covers and the general effect very clean and pleasing. The usual Sunday morning was exceptionally long. P.M.O. and I escaped church by censoring letters. Found a little more humour in this lot of letters and much more to black out. One postcard said 'If you don't get this Lil, mind you write and tell me.'

In the afternoon woken up by gun. Rushed on deck to find us chasing tramp who took no notice. Had to fire another gun before she hove to. Turned out to be Frenchman for Dunkirk. R.N.R. officers very useful for spotting nationality of these merchantmen so that Captain has one on the Bridge with him and consults him. They notice dozens of little points the R.N. officer cannot appreciate. To bed looking forward to landing, perhaps tomorrow, at St Vincent, Cape Verde Islands.

Monday October 19th. Land ahead at breakfast which soon developed into rocky volcanic islands. 8,000 ft mountains on starboard to 5,000 ft ditto to port. A dear little pointed islet crowned with a lighthouse marked the harbour of St Vincent.

As soon as we hove to we gave a salute of 21 guns to which the quaint Portuguese warship replied. The bay was filled with numerous German vessels hung up there afraid to venture out and be caught. The *Empress of Britain*, an armed merchant cruiser, was waiting for us and she put to sea at once to guard the approaches while we coaled, which we proceeded to do at once. Meanwhile, various officials boarded us including our own Consul, Captain 'Punch' Taylor. Our Captain went calling on the Governor and the Portuguese man-of-war – much scurrying of smart picket boats all over the bay.

Swarms of fruit boats and diving boys soon surround us. The collier comes alongside and we are in the filthy mess of coaling. We had our meals on the 'tween deck and shut the wardroom to keep it clean. The contractor brings us the news of the sinking of H.M.S. *Hawke*. Our Gunnery Lieutenant goes suddenly grave. It was his own ship. Being away from her at the mobilisation he was detained at another job and they filled his place on board. He is looking forward to seeing his obituary notice in the papers as his name is in the Navy List as being in the *Hawke* and it won't appear amongst the few saved therefore he *must* be dead. The islands look very bare and dry. The mountains, however, gave us a lot to look at. Very thankful for Arthur's glasses at times like these. Bought 100 oranges for 2/6 [12½p] – green, but juicy. The heat in the sun was tropical – simply scorching – and the poor beggars coaling felt it very much. They went on working from 11–3 a.m. and got in 1,300 tons. Doctors not allowed to coal, but other officers all at it and black as sweeps. In the afternoon I went ashore to get the Bill of Health. Called on the Portuguese man-of-war and found them fusing shells. They think Portuguese congress may declare war when it meets. Found the town very interesting, very dry and very empty of anything saleable. The crowd of transports etc. in here lately have bought up everything in the place. Hiring a small boy, I visited the consulate and then climbed a small peak. It was simply a cinder heap washed off the harder rocky summits round it. A fine view of a barren dried-up wilderness. A few trees, no water and no grass, only ashes and sand.

On the jetty, found a number of German sailors from the

merchant ships. They were quite willing to talk and told a dismal tale of no beer, no credit and nothing to do. Had they stayed in Buenos Aires they would be having a fine time. I saw the German Consul too, but he was shy. Only three of the ships have any coal. We won't sell any more to them and anyway it's no use. Captain tells me today we are going north again, convoying troops to England, but that we shall probably not go north of Gibraltar. The heat here intense in the sun, but a trade wind is blowing just outside the harbour and that cools us on the ship.

Coaling goes on till 3 a.m. Everything and everybody filthy black.

Tuesday October 20th. Put to sea in the afternoon fairly clean again, with two troopers behind us. The *Defence* came in before we left and coaled hurriedly. She has information *re* the *Karlsruhe* we believe, and is off with the *Carnarvon* to nab her.

Heat so bad at dinner tonight couldn't eat anything. Owing to having to have our scuttles closed to keep ship dark cannot get much ventilation.

Wednesday October 21st. A large crowd today at sick bay. The result of the heat and the coaling. At 10 a.m. the ship stopped for a few minutes for the funeral of a baby on one of the troopers. They have an epidemic on board both ships of measles, and have had several deaths. Another death at midday from enteritis. Hear today we are handing over our escort near Madeira on Saturday and return to Madeira to coal on Sunday. Delighted at prospect of seeing Funchal Bay. Doubt if I shall be lucky enough to land, however.

Thursday October 22nd. Had a very thorough practice of *General Quarters prepare for Action.* Everything ready now in our department for battle. In the afternoon rigged up a small target for air-gun practice. Was shooting against the Soldier for drinks and winning when Captain comes up and fetching his revolver blows big holes in our target. Revolver practice then became general. Fetching up my automatic I let it off at the remnant of the mark. To everyone's alarm all seven shots went off in one second like a maxim. Tried it again with the same result. Then remembered when I put it away this summer I filed the trigger to make it easier and must have done too much.

More deaths today on the transports. All the evening wonderful sheet lightning over Africa way. A new moon just showing and an oily calm sea – the ship rolling lazily to a slow swell and the air deliciously balmy and warm on deck even if stuffy below.

Friday October 23rd. This morning sighted the Canaries; high land covered with towering masses of cumulus clouds. Wrote letters and then sat down with P.M.O. and Burn to 2 hours censoring. Nothing very humorous this time except perhaps a photo postcard of Gaby Deslys sent by a man to his wife of all people. He excused the card by saying he had stolen it! This afternoon sighted Tenerife Peak 1,200 ft 114 miles away. It rose clear above the clouds around its base. Quite clear at times and at other times half hidden in the haze.

Soon after we drew up near the old *Vindictive*, which was to take our transports from us home. Our Captain went aboard her and brought back Marconi news to date, but nothing very startling. We raised a cheer when they left, and signalled good luck to them all and turning headed east for Tenerife.

Have heard from the *Marmora* that German cruiser and two transports are in the Canaries. Are to stand by in case we are wanted. This near prospect of action ought to thrill us, but it doesn't, somehow. Ship absolutely dark now at night and we may be up against the *Karlsruhe* any minute, she being reported in these waters. Tonight the Captain dined with the Ward Room Mess. Half way through dinner news came of light on the starboard bow. Captain left us for a bit and then returned and we continued dinner. Before it was over he was called to the Bridge again and one by one other officers left. Suddenly we were startled by a gun followed by another in less than a minute. Those of us left rushed on deck to find what looked like a Pacific Steam Navigation liner in the glare of our searchlights. I went on to the after-bridge and slowly we drew level with her. Her white upper-works looking very pretty in the limelight. Then our Skipper roared through the megaphone, 'Who are you?' and we could hear the relief of the steamer's crew and passengers at finding we were not a German cruiser. She was the *Orama* and after asking if she had news for us we gave her permission to go on and her passengers cheered wildly and then sang *Tipperary*. Coming over the moonlight sea – it made our fellows cheer back wildly. Redhead again disappointed at not having to board. We caught him afterwards armed with revolver, cutlas, a huge linen bag containing his boarding book and his eyeglass. He is a P. & O. 1st Officer, age 43, in peace time, short and with a merry twinkle and great favourite with the P. & O. passengers. Was on the old *Vectis* as 1st Officer after Warner's departure and disapproves of that man's flirtations. He will have to take over and command any prize we may take and we tease him about the risks he will run.

Am told by Captain we shall cruise round here for some time and possibly make for Gibraltar some time.

Saturday October 24th. Steamed along the shore of Tenerife early, and I had some fine views of the peak high above the clouds.

The crater near the summit could be seen quite well. The porphyritic rock around its edge is white and looks like snow. Above it was a little snow on the summit. The shore very rocky and precipitous, with little farmsteads perched on the top of the cliffs in little green hollows at the foot of mountainous precipices behind again. We sighted H.M.S. *Victorian* at 9 a.m. and soon drew up close to her. Captain boarded her and after that some of us made up a hurrah party and boarded her too. The Paymaster called on their 'pay' and got some fresh frozen beef as they have cold storage. We haven't such a thing, alas. I called on the P.M.O., Fleet Surgeon Hadden, an old man retired 8 years and dug up by an unkindly war. Lloyd, the Temporary Surgeon, came from Guy's. Together they had tackled an appendix and saved the man's life. They also had seen the *Carmania* whom they reported as suffering from swollen head slightly after their reception at Gibraltar. The *Victorian* is a converted Allan liner. Very sad to see the way the saloons had been gutted of all woodwork and ornaments. Most of the cabins had been pulled out of her leaving big empty spaces mournful to see. With a crew of 300 only and twice our room they were very comfortably off on board, but rather suffering from boredom after being two months stationed off Santa Cruz watching the German merchantmen sheltering there.

The rest of a perfectly beautiful day we spent boarding several ships in the vicinity, Redhead bringing back several packets of newspapers. We board everything we see now. So far no luck.

Sunday October 25th. Passed Las Palmas at 3 a.m. Came back again at 9 and anchored after chasing a Spanish ship and boarding her at 5 a.m. The usual flurry on board. Salutes and visits from the Governor, Admiral, Consul, sanitary officers, contractors, bumboats. Everything wrong today. All tiny, but cumulative effect seems great on some of the executive. Las Palmas a biggish place with trams and a harbour. 12 German and 2 Austrian vessels. Several Spanish men-of-war. It lies along the coast for several miles at the foot of sand and ash hills about 600–1,000 ft high. Above this a plain, very green and fertile, broken up by all sorts of gullies. Behind this again 8,000 ft mountains looking very bare. By a bit of luck we got ashore in the afternoon for the Bill of Health. Found my way to the Sailors Institute by accident along with the Postman. Here met by Mr and Mrs Hiley, the missionaries in charge, and given a good tea and some information, amongst which is that the Germans are still working a wireless station on the Peak at Tenerife in spite of official Spanish denials. The official classes here are stated to be strongly pro-German; very largely a question of bribery. Being Sunday afternoon all shops shut and so could buy nothing. The row back in the galley very rough. Found the Commander very excited thinking I wasn't coming back in time. Left port 5 p.m. and chased another ship. No luck and no loot.

P.S. This a.m. got a present of 8 pheasants from S.S. *Vasari* on boarding her.

Monday October 26th. Woken up this morning 2 a.m. by unusual bustle of the wireless decoders who took to jumping down the companion-way in their hurry. Soon after my cabin began to vibrate and I realised dimly we were gathering speed. Went into troubled sleep broken at intervals by the code people's jumps.

Woke to find us doing 16 knots out of sight of land S.S.E. The mystery resolved itself at breakfast. Urgent orders had reached us in the night to make for the Bissayos Islands where the *Karlsruhe* is reported. So all day we have kept up speed followed by biggish seas. A change after the calm. Burn and I performed a small operation after lunch. Exercise today took the form of skipping and for the first time this morning I tried the sail bath. Water quite warm and it's big enough to get quite a dive. Tonight as we sat in the Wardroom after dinner, the Paymaster and Padre playing the piano, the others reading and smoking quietly – myself studying J. R. Green's account of the Revolution and Charles II's reign with my legs up on the other end of the sofa as at home – the incongruity of it all came home to me again, vividly, all of us within a few hours perhaps of battle and yet apparently as remote from it in that quiet room as could be.

Tuesday October 27th. All day hurrying south at 17 knots. The weather for some reason getting cooler. We have rigged up a canvas sail bath on the shelter deck. The men use it in the evening. We have it from 7–8 a.m. It's one of the greatest treats of the day to dive into it after a stuffy, sticky night and wallow.

Wednesday October 28th. Arrived early at Dakar, an important French naval station. It has a fine harbour and a dock and is the federal capital of all the French West African colonies. Plague has been rife there lately – 3,000 deaths amongst the natives. Result, we could not land. We were coaled by negro sailors from French dockyard and gunboat. A charming young lieutenant, the Vicomte de Maupas, stayed on board and looked after them. He spoke perfect English and spoke as if he had enjoyed his year in England.

Dakar looked very clean and imposing with the large white official buildings. Above it, inland, two conical hills known as 'the Paps of Cape Verde', on one of which was the Cape Verde lighthouse. The heat was intense. In the afternoon, the *Espagne* on its way to Brazil, came in and anchored close to. It's a splendid liner and carried passengers. Every officer on board who could spare a minute found his way to the quarter-deck to gaze with glasses at some of the girls on board who were waving to us. Starved as we are of all feminine society the sight of Parisian frocks proved too much for the dignity of several. The middies got quite excited and quarrelled over who should have the next turn at the glasses. To me the babies on board were as interesting as a very pretty Brazilian who was flirting desperately with an officer of the *Espagne* round a corner away from the other passengers. Our Captain went on board her and came back quite excited over the beauty of her fittings and furniture. Left at 7 p.m. in chase of the *Karlsruhe* again.

Thursday October 29th. Going dead slow this morning feeling our way in towards the mouth of the river near the Islands, the lead being heaved all the time. Suddenly we got a wireless to say *Karlsruhe* reported 50 miles south of Dakar on night of 26–27th. So we had missed her. We anchored nearly all day and waited for further news and instructions. This news had come from the *Highflyer*. Luckily the sun was hidden behind a haze all day so that it didn't get unbearably hot. We rigged up a shark hook in the afternoon and after tea the sharks began to come round. Two large 7–8 footers and a number of babies. Once or twice they sniffed at the bait but no luck. Still it was interesting watching them. In the morning we had revolver practice. Fired myself about 30–40 rounds and improved a good deal.

This evening has been one of the pleasantest of the whole voyage. The Captain brought up his gramophone on deck and we all sat round the quarter-deck in the tropical moonlight listening to a varied selection. After a time a few couples started dancing. Stewart, the A.P, yclept Mossy Face on account of his sprouting beard, Redhead of the P. & O. and Burn the Temporary Surgeon and the Commander being amongst the best. I lay out at length on my grass-mat, bought at Dakar, with a pillow for my elbow and listened dreamily to the music and conversation, my thoughts very far away at times.

Said the Gunnery Lieutenant suddenly, apropos nothing, 'How many many times this is better than the North Sea.' No one contradicted him. Later I brought a blanket up and tried sleeping on deck. It was easier than I thought and I dosed fitfully until a tropical shower at 3 a.m. drove all of us on deck into our stuffy cabins.

Friday October 30th. Cruising about quietly all day until we met the *Highflyer* in the evening as arranged by wireless. She is a very old tubby cruiser. We watched her with interest. She had made history by sinking the *Kaiser Wilhelm der Grosse*. Heard details of the affair which were rather more lengthy than we had thought. Apparently they started signalling to each other at 9,000 yards.

The K.W. said, 'Of course you will respect Spain's neutrality?'

The H.'s reply was, 'You have been there 5 days and are evidently making it a base. Come out and fight or we shall shell you.'

Reply to this was, 'Had not we better refer the whole matter to the Spanish Governor?'

H. replied, 'Be blowed to you. We give you two hours to decide and we advise you to send all non-combatants on to your colliers off the ship to avoid loss of life.'

This they did. At the end of the time the *Highflyer* asked them to surrender again. Answer was, 'Germans don't surrender.' Then the battle began. The H. was hit 5 times before she got one on the German and she fired some 600 rounds altogether. The thing which sank her [the *Kaiser Wilhelm der Grosse*] was a shell hole on the waterline aft which was enormously large. The range was 9,000 yards – very far for old-type 6-inch guns . . .

She looked as if she was making things as comfortable as possible on board. A shark hook hung from her admiral's walk and the quarter-deck was littered with armchairs. Our Captain went aboard her.

Saturday October 31st. Proceeding quietly north in company with *Highflyer*, overhauling several ships *en route*. All British – no luck except a few newspapers, some cucumbers and papaws. Our ice has run out and we long for cold drinks again. Put a spinning spoon overboard on the end of a line all day, but no bites. In the evening again had dancing by moonlight, the ship stationary. Meanwhile the *Highflyer* has gone on to Dakar to bring us some ships to convoy. General impression is we are bound for Sierra Leone. Below are the names of a few steamers we have recently overhauled.

Orama (P.S.N.Co.), *Ancobra* (Jonathan Holt), *Ariadne-Irene* (N.Z.S.Co.).

Sunday November 1st. Started this evening for Sierra Leone. Expect to reach it Tuesday daylight.

Monday November 2nd. Distinctly hotter. The flying fishes playing in shoals all around us. Porpoises chasing them and then diving under the ship. This afternoon passed a small whaler with its barrel of a crow's-nest very dirty, very small and unlike anything else afloat. Driven off the deck at 2 a.m. by a tropical downpour, the first real rain for months.

Tuesday November 3rd. Norah's[2] birthday. Arrived Freetown, Sierra Leone at daybreak. I was much impressed with the first views of the place. It's very hilly, thickly wooded and very green. The harbour is very large – an estuary in fact, and on the south shore stands Freetown. Imagine a horseshoe of green wooded hills, about 2,000 ft at the centre, sloping down to the sea. In the middle of this amphitheatre, enclosed, a smaller hill about 500 ft. The town clusters all around this hill on the summit of which is situated the barracks and mess of one of the regiments. On the high hills at the background are numerous bungalows and barracks. Behind these hills can be seen the highest peak in the place, the Sugarloaf, 3,000 ft. Close to our anchorage we found the *Marmora*, a converted P. & O. After breakfast I took all our sick over to her where they stayed the two days while we coaled. The P.M.O. was Fleet Surgeon Iliewicz, an old S.S.M.[3] boy. We talked about the old school over a deliciously cold drink. Poor man, he had retired – married just two years – and was dug up. Very worried he was at the chances of the *Marmora* in a fight. They had operated successfully on a case of appendicitis – he and Walker from Glasgow. Coming away our boat carried away their companion ladder much to the rage of the officer of the day whose language was dreadful. After lunch Burn and I went ashore. We wandered up to the summit of the 500 ft hill, intensely interested in the population. The dear old creole women in their voluminous print dresses, the more scantily dressed negroes from inland and the dandies who wore *one* trouser leg turned up to the knee and the other full length, real knuts in bowler hats and velour shirts. We dug out a coloured tailor and ordered some whites and then descended in search of a drink. However, we met the Captain at a loose end and so we wandered round the town with him until evening. The ship so filthy with coal dust. I took my mat and slept up on the Bridge, very nice and cool.

2 Surgeon Dixon's wife, Norah Dixon, who was pregnant at the time.
3 School for the Sons of Missionaries.

Wednesday November 4th. Leave for all officers and 300 of the men after coaling. I went ashore early and bought a helmet 11/6 [57½p], a deck chair for 8/– [40p] and a few fish hooks. Took a few snaps, was stalking a fine group of piccaninnies when the mother rushed out and snatched them all in doors. Then she came out very excitedly and shrieked 'You pay? No pay no photograph'. My retort was I had got them and as she was so greedy and mistrustful she shouldn't have anything.

Up to the club to lunch where the cold drinks were much appreciated. Saw the washerwomen washing our whites we had entrusted to them. They came aboard yesterday, dear old women in amazingly ample clothes and tapped at our cabin as we were all getting up. Knowing the P.M.O. was in his bath I sent Mrs Amelia Smith to collar his contract. She came back indignant. 'You know he was in his bath,' she said. 'You ver' naughty man.' After more shopping some of us took the afternoon train up to Hill Station. The train runs through the streets of Sierra Leone quite un-guarded, and climbs up the hill sides for half an hour to about 800 ft, carrying with it all the civil officials to their bungalows. Each as he got in had handed to him his slip of wireless news (Reuter). The Soldier and No. 1 stopped at Barracks Station and called on the Mess. The Padre and I went to the top. Here, as we were feeling a little lost, the Deputy Comptroller of the Treasury, a Mr Hamilton, invited us to tea and we accepted gratefully. His bungalow was one of twenty other exactly-similar ones in a fair-sized garden and built on high piers. The soil of the garden had been carried up from the town as it is very rocky up here. Hamilton's wife and ten-month baby live at Wellow and he is alone out here. After tea, such tea too after ships' stuff, we walked up to the point and got a glorious view of mountains, sea and town. A ship lay wrecked on the Carpenter rocks below us, sitting so well that it was difficult to believe that she was not anchored. The gardens were full of bougainvillaea, hibiscus, convolvulus, rhododendrons and many others we could not find a name for. Before leaving, he gave us a tablet of coal-tar soap each (we had tried to get some in the town and failed) and a packet of mustard and cress seeds for the P.M.O. as from one gardener to another. We said goodbye at the station, he walking down as far, through the tennis courts and groups of people sitting out after their games. On board again I found the washing had returned but no fresh whites. An enquiry found that the Officer of the Watch had noticed a man trying to get aboard shouting out 'Dixie'. So he told him to go back there, and my whites went back to the tailor – the tragedy being that they were paid for! We sent urgent messages back to the washerwomen but at 9 p.m. a violent thunderstorm commenced and lasted till we were at sea after midnight. *Experientia docet*[4].

Thursday November 5th. Steaming $17\frac{1}{2}$ knots S.W. bound for Brazil 6 days to Abrolhos Rocks where we are to coal from collier. The ship vibrates at this speed. Hear that 3 men have deserted and we have given their description to the *Marmora*. One man is in my stretcher party and I have had to get the stout canteen contractor to take his place.

Friday November 6th. Meeting the S.E. trade winds now. It's quite cool – in fact cold – in the wind and the sea is distinctly choppy. The nearer we get to the equator the rougher and colder it gets. We are quite off any trade route and haven't seen a steamer since we left. Have been feeling headachy and sick for two days and shaky all the time. Partly the sun at Sierra Leone I think.

Saturday November 7th. Crossed the line at 10.56 this evening. Had an equatorial sweepstake on the time we should cross. Foreman, Lt. Eng., won £2.10s [£2.50], the only prize. Today discovered and invented a new game. It's a sort of Badminton tennis, played over a rope $4\frac{1}{2}$ ft high with a big sort of football stuffed with sand and padded weighing about 20 lb. No racquets – we catch the ball before it reaches the ground. It's most strenuous and every muscle in my body ached after two games. But it's going to revolutionise the exercise question for me on board. Is a most exciting game and owing to the ball used, called Ping Pong.

Sunday November 8th. Gradually getting out of the S.E. trades and the sea getting calmer and the sun hotter. The evenings are still delightful and as a rule I sit out in my deck chair often and talk to the Captain who seems to enjoy company, after the day's official austerity, in which to unbend.

4   *Experience teaches.*

Monday November 9th. Lost the trade winds. The midday sun about as nearly vertically above as it can be. Ping Pong increasing in favour. The Captain relaxes the vigour of the censorship and says we can mention equator, Sierra Leone. Nothing to cross out therefore this evening as we sat, four of us, P.M.O., Burn, myself and the Postman stewing in the 1st Cabin reading the very guarded effusions of the Scottish mind under suspicion that everything is read by 'that wretched censor'.

My Lux is running short. Shall miss it.

Tuesday November 10th. A quiet day getting ready for hand coaling.

Wednesday November 11th. Anchored early this morning near the Abrolhos Rocks, Brazil, but just out of sight of them. Met two colliers. The *Thistleton* came alongside and bumped a hole in our fo'c'sle, carried away some davits and other minor damage. By 9 a.m. we were in the thick of it again. This business of coaling merits a description. On the day all officers turn up at breakfast in most weird costumes. The Wardroom is closed and breakfast served between decks. In an hour decks are inches deep in coal dust. Men and officers are as black as colliers and eventually everything tastes, smells and feels coal. We had, today, to take in 1,300 tons. The coal is dug out of the collier's hold by a party from the *Kent,* put into bags holding 2 cwt each and slung up 10 at a time on to the *Kent*'s deck, the noise of the donkey engines being appalling. Here the bags are unhooked and each is seized and put into wheelbarrows, and men race off down the decks to the chutes with them, where they are tipped into chutes and so into the bunkers. In these bunkers men are engaged in trimming it *i.e.* shovelling it into the out-of-the-way corners and generally putting as much as possible into the smallest possible space. This latter is an appalling job. An easy calculation shows that we have taken on today 13,000 bags. Almost every man in the ship has worked unremittingly in the tropical heat from 6 a.m. till 11 p.m. The officers whack in as hard as the men and snatch hurried meals as they are. The sight of 20 filthy black people trying to eat a civilised dinner after coaling all day is weird in the extreme: the discomfort of it has to be felt before it can be realised. Everything down below, cabins and all get covered with a layer of black which remains for two or three days and spoils any attempt at keeping our whites clean. And just as soon as the ship is clean again another coaling comes. If we steam fast we have to coal every five–six days.

After dinner today I obtained the P.M.O.'s permit to coal. Doctors are not allowed to really, as we are supposed to keep clean and ready for accidents. First tried 'tipping' *i.e.* lifting the bags and emptying them down the chutes. After a few hundred times my muscles called for a change so annexing my servant's barrow, much to this stout old gentleman's relief, I rushed several dozen cwt along, dodging the other barrows and a hundred other obstructions and finally waited my turn on the hot quarter-deck for refills. This palling, I got the Engineer Lieutenant to conduct me into a bunker. Imagine a space 30 by 15 ft with sloping floor and you have the upper bunker. The floor slopes down to a sliding door into the lower bunkers. The coal is dropped into the upper bunkers and owing to the slope much of it finds its way unaided into the lower. Here again it has to be helped into various out-of-the-way corners by the trimmers. We entered through a door into the upper bunker and took small smoky lamps with us. The dust is thick and choking and the light is invisible at 6 ft away. One's lungs refuse to breathe the thick stuff at first and you cough and choke in it. Feeling our way we dropped through the hole into the lower bunker. Here the dust and heat were worse still. Men were at work here stowing the coal under a shelf. I never saw them I only heard them, though they were only 6 ft away. I had had enough and started to ascend. Just then some fool above started pouring in coal from above. Foreman shouted to me from below to tell him to stop. I could hear the stuff thundering down and lumps were hitting me. I tried to get near the chute; more and more coal came pouring down. The air was almost solid now with dust: my lamp was out and visions of being buried under the avalanche loomed very big. My shouts were drowned in the general roar. Seriously alarmed, I found myself jammed into a corner, unable to get out and expecting every minute to be crushed to death. If only I could have seen. Feeling about desperately I found myself under another chute, which was not being used luckily, or I should have been killed and succeeded in attracting someone's attention up above. The fire ceased and I escaped. The stokers of the Navy deserve far more of their country than they get poor beggars, especially in war time.

After tea I tried digging coal in the depth of the collier. The digging wasn't so bad but the choking dust drove me off. I essayed unhooking. After nearly breaking my fingers and narrowly escaping being knocked overboard I retired. The subsequent attempts to get clean in a hip bath were pathetically ineffective.

The *Edinburgh Castle* (armoured cruiser) kept guard for us. She hadn't had a mail since she left England in September and her food supply was poor. She transferred twenty boys to us. Where they are to go in our overcrowded vessel is a mystery. We intercepted a wireless message from the Abrolhos Lighthouse saying that colliers were in the neighbourhood and probably this was a British rendezvous. Thus everywhere we go our movements are instantly sent to German agents who keep their cruisers informed. We leave tonight at midnight for Monte Video. The sun today at noon was exactly overhead . . .

Thursday November 12th. This afternoon sighted the R.M.S.P. S.S. *Amazon*. She refused to stop until we fired two guns. Her passengers cheered us repeatedly and a party of volunteers for the war who were on board gave us a bugle call salute. Our mails were to have gone with the boarding boat, but the Postman lost his chance and now our letters will probably reach home fourteen days later. I cursed the wretched man heartily. The *Amazon*'s Captain was irate at being stopped. He grumbled at losing an hour, 'Why didn't we use our wireless if we wanted information?' However, we got from her some fresh frozen meat, fruit, ice, jam and herrings amongst other things and also the sickening news that the *Good Hope* and *Monmouth* (our sister ship) were sunk by the *Scharnhorst* and *Gneisenau* off Valparaiso[5]. All the news is obviously German in origin and we still hope against hope it can't be true. There is a mystery somewhere we look forward to getting explained. General feeling is that we shall now get into the Pacific in chase. But the result tonight of everything – the reaction of coaling, bad news, missing the post; is that everyone is serious and depressed.

5   The Battle of Coronel.

Friday November 13th. We are a crippled old ship, owing to being rushed out before our engine room was really efficient. We are now unable to condense water quickly enough and therefore cannot steam more than 10 knots. So we crawl south when every minute is precious if we are to be in at the death of the Pacific marauders. Our electric supply too is very independable; it varies in strength constantly and is for ever going out when it's most wanted *e.g.* at firing practice or General Quarters. Everyone inventing theories to account for the loss of the *Good Hope* and *Monmouth*.

Saturday November 14th. Astonished on getting up this morning to find sun coming in by porthole. Must be going north again obviously. Explanation forthcoming very soon. Wireless came last night from the *Defence* ordering us to proceed to Abrolhos at 8 knots. She herself coming up north at 12 knots. Something must have happened off Chile. Can the Japanese have taken on the *Gneisenau* etc., or are they already sunk or interned. General feeling is they must have been so damaged that they couldn't get out of Valparaiso in time and interned.

Heavy rain this afternoon. After it was all over we put out every available tin and bath and sail tank: has refused to rain since. After tea we had our first taste of full charge 6-inch gun firing. We went to General Quarters for it. That meant purgatory down below for the medical parties, while the crew above enjoyed watching the fun. However, I crept up after a bit and was in time to see the target shot away at 5,000 yards, much to the mingled pride and disgust of the gunners because it meant making another target and getting away from it again. The shooting was very good and has done the ship's company a lot of good. They will go into action now confident they can sink anything in five minutes. The Gunnery Lieutenant all smiles.

A word as to what General Quarters means. It means going to our positions ready for battle. In our case the P.M.O. and I go down to the fore-cross passage below the waterline and just over the magazine. The whole space is filled with perspiring men heaving up ammunition and shells from the magazines up the hoist into the casemates above. In addition, there is a steering wheel and compass with a steering party, spare electricians, messengers, ambulance parties, sick bay attendants and transmitters, etc., etc. Situated just in front, as it is, of the boilers the temperature there usually exceeds 100° and sometimes goes up to 115°. We sweat streams and gasp for air when the fan stops as it sometimes does. What it will be like in real action no one who has not had experience can imagine.

Sunday November 15th. A very uneventful day. 'Medicine ball' in the afternoon: a species of tennis played with a 20 lb football over a 4 ft net.

Monday November 16th. In the afternoon sighted a ship in distance. Signal bo'sun had the name wrong and we were going to pass her. Luckily we didn't and she turned out to be the *Ortega* (P.S.N.Co.). She had mails for us. The passengers raised a fine cheer as we drew alongside and some person with a cornet kept playing the National Anthem in a most quaint manner. The sight of women and children again affecting most of us. After dinner the P.M.O. and I strolled on the quarter-deck for an hour and when at last I got below was delighted to get a letter from my wife dated Oct 25th, evidently the latest mail possible. Delighted to find she is keeping so well. Newspapers up to Oct 29th. We all sat round the wardroom in silence for about 2 hours reading furiously to get up to date. Everyone very happy at getting mails at last.

Tuesday November 17th. Anchored close off Abrolhos Island and lighthouse early. Find there *Edinburgh Castle* and two colliers. Started to coal 9 a.m. I fished with no success, then went to the conning tower and started to chip paint off it. This set a fashion and getting tools the P.M.O., Burn, Pay[6] and a boy started seriously to work, hammering off the thick paint of years. This is being done all over the ship as a prevention against fire. After lunch the *Defence*, *Carnarvon* and *Cornwall* hove to along with the *Otranto* and *Orama*. The sea was soon busy with picket boats and sailing galleys flying from ship to ship. Admiral Stoddart in the *Defence* is now our head and we are awaiting reinforcements in the shape of the *Inflexible* and *Invincible*. The news of the *Good Hope* and *Monmouth* is only too

6   Paymaster Andrews.

true. The Germans came up from the west with the sun behind them (*No, just the reverse [*added later*]) and our poor fellows shooting into the sun couldn't see where their shots were going. It was rough and so we couldn't use our lower deck guns. The *Otranto* fled. The *Canopus* is at Falkland Islands defending them. German Fleet expected up here possibly in chase of us now that they have tasted blood. At dinner, more mails were brought from the *Otranto*, being the first letters sent out really. Also piles of newspapers. Commander Williams and Surgeon Trench came over from the *Carnarvon*. The latter I knew at Haslar[7] two years ago. We more or less abandoned dinner to read our letters, dirty and black as we all were. Afterwards more thirst quenching than at any other coaling so far. A very merry crew after. I have undertaken the editorship of the *Kent Kronikal* published monthly. It will mean a lot of work and *tact*. Material is coming in but it will need redrawing and retyping owing to our method of reproduction by gelatine pad.

Wednesday November 18th. Everyone late and with sore heads, but cheerful. The censors delayed with a sudden mail to go via *Edinburgh Castle*. Went over to her on the forage but couldn't get much. Took over four sick people to return to England, including the Engineer Lieutenant Commander with gastric ulcer, and a man who got his face smashed in yesterday at coaling and on whom we operated to some success. The *Edinburgh Castle* all glitter gold and carpets! Not fitted like other armed cruisers. We felt like Pirates boarding Paradise. The huge decks, the awnings, cold drinks and general air of comfort and elegance made one *half* wish had been appointed to her instead of the *Kent*. But on second thoughts no. I wanted to experience what a 'battleship' life meant.

After lunch, we took on guard and steamed out of harbour, to patrol up and down outside and protect the place while the others coal. We fired two torpedoes. The first fired by No. 1 from the Bridge fizzed and suddenly, from beneath where I stood, leapt into the air and then went fizzling away towards the target two thousand yards away. I could plainly see its track and suddenly it hit the target and came to the surface. The Holmes light burnt and

7   Naval Hospital at Portsmouth.

a thick cloud of smoke went up showing where it was to the boat waiting to pick it up. The target was only 4 ft square and to hit it was great work. But our Torpedo Lieutenant was No. 1 at *Vernon* – the torpedo school – and so ought to know something about them. The second torpedo fired by telephone by Redhead wasn't so good but I was able to secure a photo. Had some fun with baby sharks. Just as we were about to catch one the screw turned and scared them.

Are living on one-hour-west time, instead of South American time or real time. The result is we are over an hour and a half earlier than in reality. The effect is a sort of 'Daylight Saving Bill'. We get up before it's got too hot and we dine at night in daylight with the scuttles open and get a cool dinner.

Tonight, as I was writing this diary, suddenly comes a messenger to all our cabins. Go to Action Stations. Instantly in the dark hundreds of people moving all over the place, quickly turning out of their hammocks and running silently to spots assigned. Five minutes later we were all sent back to our bunks by bugle. The explanation rather funny. Captain wished to test his buglers and see if they sounded off quick enough on the order having been given from the bridge. People were stationed near the unsuspecting buglers to stop them actually doing it and so rousing the crew. However, the order on the bridge was overheard in the transmitting station down in the bowels of the ship and instantly passed along to the guns which were thrown loose by the crews in no time and by word of mouth the whole ship was aroused and down at their stations before Captain could stop us. A splendid show everyone agrees.

Saturday November 28th. Much has happened since I wrote last. On one of our days outside Abrolhos we fired our 6-inch guns at a target towed by the *Carnarvon*. Our shooting was rotten. Life at Abrolhos was very interesting to me at any rate. The *Bristol* came in from Bahia with mails up to Nov 4th. The *Glasgow* arrived from Rio having remedied her holes got in the battle of Valparaiso. Some of us boarded her. Apparently the hole in her after compartment threatened to bulge in the armoured deck below and seriously reduced her speed. Therefore her Captain decided to clear out as he only had short-range torpedoes. She had five wounded. One by one, various colliers steamed in and took up stations and lastly Admiral Sturdee with the *Inflexible* and the *Invincible* (dreadnought battle cruisers). Everyone's spirits cheered up at once on their arrival (Thursday November 26th). They looked fine. Colliers went alongside them soon after arrival and they took in about 1,500 tons each. Meanwhile we fraternised. The *Invincible* brought us mails up to Nov 9th and the *Inflexible* one month's provisions. We were very busy all day Friday taking in stores, including some beer from the *Inflexible* of which we have had none for weeks.

Fishing has been very popular, but with no great success aft. The crew caught some fine bream. The big 40 lb rock cod though, didn't come our way.

One day we blew off some gun-cotton charges under water and picked up the stunned garfish by the dozen from boats, and got wet through and nearly sea sick it was so rough.

The Fleet assembled here is an imposing sight, I expect, to the Abrolhosians. It comprises: *Invincible*, (flag ship), *Inflexible*, *Defence*, *Carnarvon*, *Cornwall*, *Kent*, *Bristol*, *Glasgow*, *Orama* and ten or eleven colliers and a supply ship the *Crown of Bangor*. It's not unduly hot with the breeze.

The Fleet sailed today, south for the Falkland Islands, except the *Defence*, which goes to St Helena. It was to me a fascinating sight to see ship after ship leave her moorings and take her position in line. By the afternoon, however, we could only see one ship on the horizon, the others all at their stations over fifty miles of sea.

Sunday November 29th. Gorgeous weather. The *Carnarvon* is on our port beam. The battle cruisers are out of sight behind the *Carnarvon* and in the middle of the fleet, which is sweeping a fifty mile path, the *Bristol* has gone into Rio for news and to take our letters. Have been very busy with the Commander and the P.M.O. getting out the *Abrolhos Advertiser*, worrying out jokes, printing on a typewriter with hectograph ink and then getting fifty copies off from the gelatine which had first to be frozen in the ice chest. It has meant any amount of work.

Monday November 30th. Heavy gun firing today, at a target which the *Carnarvon* towed for us and we in turn for them. Our firing very good. Fired 144 rounds. Total value over £2,000 in a few minutes. The *Carnarvon*'s first salvo came very near our stern and ricocheted whining over our heads. We didn't like it at all. Admiral Stoddart on the *Carnarvon* has the reputation of being a fool. He is alleged to have had the *Karlsruhe* within 15 miles of him and when information of the fact was brought to him he first ordered immediate pursuit – she was coaling up a river off Brazil – then changed his mind and said he had been ordered to Abrolhos and went on. His officers fell in and almost mutinied over it. Thank God he is no longer in command of the fleet. Sturdee has a fine reputation. Wireless message from Monte to say enemy seen 400 miles off Rio! Everyone *very* cheerful.

Tuesday December 1st. After working hard all day produced the *Kronikal* at 9 p.m., this evening. The reception it had was most flattering – better than I had ever hoped for. Just as we were binding up the copies a wireless message came. Merchant ship in danger of capture, and giving her position. We altered course at once and worked up to full speed. Everyone on quarter-deck eagerly discussing the news and very happy over it. Thought it might be the *Kronprinz Wilhelm* which is an armoured cruiser known to be in these waters. We were all turning in prepared to be called to action in the night when orders came from flagship to resume our course and stations again. It turned out to be a code mistake.

Wednesday December 2nd. Sea rough and big swell. Much cooler and we have gone back into blue clothes again. Felt a little sick all day, and missed lunch. Better tonight. The moon full and perfectly lovely tonight on the tossing sea. The paint chipping fever very strong. All officers engaged this afternoon in clearing the after turret with hammers. It's not a bad game whacking the paint off but it's hard work. I distinguished myself by making a large scale map of the British Isles and Continent on the turret. It took over ten thousand chips of the hammer I reckoned.

Tuesday December 3rd. One of the most perfect days of the voyage. The sea quite calm again and the sun warm like an English summer day. Paint chipping all the rage, this morning half a dozen officers engaged at it on the after turret. Everyone cheerful. Heard by wireless from the Falklands. This evening perfectly lovely. Everyone on deck after dinner and skylarking like boys, while the moon came up full. The P. and O. armed cruiser *Macedonia* has joined our fleet. Behind me in the next cabin five officers are having a supper; caviare and champagne. They are just getting cheerful.

Friday December 4th. Perhaps the most perfect day from the weather point of view we have yet had. A touch of cold in the air, a strong breeze and a rolling sea flecked with white horses. The nip in the air has given a zest to all our doings. Saw our first albatrosses today. Such lovely great things floating along at 40 miles an hour. Several whales sighted spouting. Spent all day chipping paint off the turret – just an excuse to keep up in the fresh air. The ship rolling grandly all day. The Assistant Paymaster showed today!

Saturday December 5th. This morning cold, raining and misty. Up on deck, if I shut my eyes I could smell Swiss mists and smell the cold air off a glacier. I spent all the morning in a reverie climbing over again the old climbs – but especially recalling bivouacs among the mists. In the afternoon the fog I had smelt came and for half an hour all gun crews had to go to their guns in case we came upon the enemy suddenly. This spoilt the chance of holding the loader competition upon which the officers had a sweepstake – the auction of which was held at lunch and was most amusing. This evening clear and cold, the *south* wind very cold. Still paint chipping. Amusing to see the Commander and No. 1 absorbed, deeply absorbed, in chipping out a Chinese dragon on the after shelter deck. Shades of ye commanders of ten years ago.

BATTLE OF THE FALKLANDS

Monday December 7th. Arrived Port Stanley in the Falklands and proceeded immediately to coal, the *Kent* excepted – we had to keep steam up and coal last and follow up the fleet when we could. The Admiral was in a hurry to get round Cape Horn. The *Kent* will probably proceed through the Straits of Magellan to meet the battle cruisers who would go round the Cape. Very cold, windy and raining in squalls. Beastly weather.

Tuesday December 8th.[*First entry, written at the time*] 8 a.m. Just heard two cruisers seen at sea. Are putting out to sea at once in chase, the other ships to follow. Everyone busy preparing for battle. Very kind of them to come here and save us the trouble of going round the Horn to find them.

[*Second entry, written later*] Was late in rising and heard the astonishing news at breakfast. Could hardly believe it, and wasn't worried but took the precaution of putting my valuables in a box ready to take below. We put to sea at once. As we passed the flagship she sounded off 'Clear for Action', and the crew were very busy throwing off the collier. As we got out near the harbour entrance I could see the smoke of two ships on our starboard over a low-lying ridge of sand. Suddenly the *Canopus* – anchored in the inner harbour – fired two shots over the intervening low hill by means of her observation post on the hill. I was told afterwards the first shots fell short by a long way but that her third round – one of them ricocheted and hit the *Gneisenau*. I was on A2 casemate and saw the two cruisers shoot round the point, alter course, and flee away as hard as they could S.E. A prisoner told me afterward they never had such a shock in their lives as when they got 12-inch shots land near them from apparently nowhere, and then rounding the point saw a whole squadron of ships including, they were amazed to see, battle cruisers.

Soon after we cleared the harbour and saw three more cruisers on the horizon. The two that came in to spy were the *Gneisenau* and the *Nürnberg*. We pelted after the enemy and soon after there came out behind us the two battle cruisers (*Invincible* and *Inflexible*), followed by *Glasgow* and *Cornwall*, and a long way behind the *Carnarvon* with the *Bristol* and *Macedonia*. The latter two steamed off towards the west to capture the enemy's colliers. It was a fine sight, the big dreadnoughts tearing up with their black smoke against a background of blue sea and the mountains behind that again. For a wonder too the day was calm with bright sunshine, though the wind was bitterly cold.

The *Kent* was very short of coal and had only a day and a half's supply at full speed. We were cutting up all the wooden ladders, targets, etc., and sending the bits to the stokehold to burn. Everyone was amazingly cheerful and confident, joking as they prepared for action. I took several photos of officers on the quarter-deck and of the flagship tearing past us. At eleven o'clock we had a picnic lunch in the flooded Wardroom on a sodden tablecloth but we eat heartily. The control top officers were all in thick duffel 'North Sea' gun crew jackets. We were then 11 a.m., doing 22 knots! and slowed down for the battle cruisers to pass us. After they did everyone went forward onto the fo'c'sle to watch. I took a seat on the top of the fore turret and wrote a hurried diary of events with a few diagrams of the positions of the vessels at certain times. I also went up on the Bridge and took a photo of the Captain on the Bridge. The Germans had strung out after a twelve miles' start into line abreast.

At 12.53 one of our big ones opened fire. A roar of cheers went up from our crew as they saw the smoke and flash. The shots fell short of the last German in the line (the *Dresden*). It was wonderful after this to watch the battle, sitting out on the turret in the sunshine, with a cheering crowd of sailors beneath. In ten minutes shots from the *Inflexible* were straddling the *Dresden* and suddenly we saw her turn to starboard and make off hard. Our crew sent up a howl of derision. The battle cruisers then commenced firing at No. 4 and she turned away after the *Dresden* – she was the *Leipzig*, followed by the *Nürnberg* who was No. 1 in their line.

At 1.30 the *Scharnhorst* and *Gneisenau* opened fire and it was a pretty sight, their guns all going off together beautifully and their first shots fell very near our big 'uns but short. A minute or two later they suddenly turned hard to port towards the *Inflexible* and *Invincible* firing for all they were worth. Action sounded off then and we had to go to our stations, but I got a photo just before I went of the battle cruisers in a pall of smoke as we passed them on our port beam, we on our chase of the three German light cruisers.

At 2.54 we were allowed on deck again. On our port horizon we could just see the *Inflexible* and *Invincible* firing at the Germans and could see the German shots dropping round our ships. The Germans altered course to port again to get nearer to their tormentors, but our ships followed suit and soon all we could see was faint smoke.

Meanwhile we had been slowly overhauling the light cruisers ahead of us. The *Glasgow* had moved across from our port to our starboard bow. The *Cornwall* was on our starboard beam. The *Leipzig*, the centre one of the three Germans, had lagged behind and at 2.56 we were surprised to hear the guns of the *Glasgow* open fire – her shots fell short. The *Leipzig* replied, also short. The next hour was wonderfully exciting. I had never expected to see a battle so close. The *Glasgow* and the *Leipzig* booming off at each other at long range but the fall of shot easily visible. Our crew went to tea before 4 o'clock and I got mine in the sick bay with the stewards, giving them a box of biscuits as my share of the feast. On the Bridge again at 4 p.m.; firing now in deadly earnest both sides. But there was an interval of 30 seconds between the flash of the guns and the fall of the shot and the interval seemed ages when holding glasses to one's eyes waiting to see the result.

We were steadily overhauling the *Leipzig* ourselves and so was the *Cornwall*. Suddenly I saw a flash of flame on the far side of the *Leipzig* – evidently one of the *Glasgow*'s salvos had taken effect and our crew cheered wildly. Shots were falling all around the *Glasgow* however and we felt sure she must be getting hit too. We also wondered why she didn't leave the *Leipzig* to us and go after the

Dresden ahead of her and going away hard too.

At 4.20 the *Leipzig* suddenly turned to port, evidently to give us the benefit of a broadside. We turned off, too, to port. The *Cornwall* turned off to starboard and so we had her between us, but ahead. Action sounded and just as I turned to go below our fore turret opened fire beneath me and made me jump. Down below everything was very quiet. We heard about eight salvos fired and then news came down to us that we had passed the *Leipzig* and were pursuing the *Nürnberg*, course S.57E.; and that the weather had turned slightly rainy and misty. We prayed that she shouldn't escape in fog.

At 5.15 we heard the fore turret guns go off and knew we had overhauled her. At 5.25 Commander came down to us to say she had dropped a shell beyond us, *i.e.* we were within range of her guns too. Also that the other ships out of view so that it is ship to ship now. At 5.30 I find a note in the log that we are firing our starboard and bow guns, and that the paint is falling in flakes from the 'ceiling'!

The sailors and marines around me very cheerful and jesting quietly. Marshall, in B1 casemate, sends down word shells are dropping over us into the sea on his side, the sheltered one. The Commander came down and told us we were 8,000 yards.

I went along aft to see if Burn's party were alright and found them serious but safe. Foreman came down along the passage soon after with a fine piece of shell he had picked up on deck. The noise at this time was terrific, all our starboard guns firing, and occasionally a crash followed by tinkling noises told us we were hit ourselves.

At 5.30 the demand came down for lyddite shell instead of ordinary. A cheer greeted the news as we knew then we must be hitting her properly. Same time someone shouts down that she is on fire – terrific cheers. Range then 4,300 yards. At 6 p.m. felt a bad hit – terrific crash followed by a blast of air, felt right in the port ammunition passages.

The demand then came along for medical assistance for wounded man in compartment just above the fore-cross passage. I went up, followed by Bilben the S.B. steward and in the dim light found a man with a shell splinter which had entered his back and gone through his chest and was lying just under the skin of his left breast. Gave him morphia and placed a dressing on the wound. Just then a shell came through the ship's side on the deck above us. We were blown backwards, dazed for a second with noise and flash and there was a filthy smell of lyddite. The whole place seemed tumbling about our ears. A heavy iron grating fell from the upper deck on to the ladder above my head and added to the noise. No one hurt in the compartment. I finished the dressing – left him in charge of two of his mates – and fled below again. The case was hopeless.

The fore passage shook again and again to explosions which seemed just above our heads. We had closed down to 3,000 yards I heard afterwards. Two badly burnt men came down to us after this and we heard how a shell had come into the A3 casemate, set fire to the cordite there and every man in the casemate was burnt, one man being dead. The Paymaster and I dressed them, gave them morphia, and they lay down in the passage suffering from shock. Meanwhile the *Kent* had cross the bows of the *Nürnberg* steering in a large curve about 4,000 yards away from the *Nürnberg* and was pouring in lyddite. Then we turned to port to give the starboard guns crews a rest and the others a chance. Down below we went over to the starboard side therefore and found the passage running with water which had come down from A3 in the efforts to put the fire out. Sergeant Mayes did an act here which I hope will get him the V.C. A flaming cordite charge came down the hoist with a sheet of flame. The ammunition party retreated at once. The sergeant, however, seized the flaming cordite and threw it clear of the other cordite lying in the passage and then closed the watertight doors, thus saving an explosion and severe fire[8]. Then came Kelly, a marine with his legs both blown off. Bilben had gone up and attended to him *in situ* first and had brought him down. I took his dying message to his wife and gave morphia. He was unconscious and moribund a few minutes after.

Down below we had no idea how the fight was really going. Up above they knew early in the fight we were top dog. It was a great relief then to hear the guns cease fire suddenly. We waited for ten minutes. News came that she was sinking and badly on fire. Suddenly a shell hit us again and we opened fire in return for five

8   Sergeant Mayes was awarded the Conspicuous Gallantry Medal.

minutes again. Then the news came she has hauled down her flag. We waited at our posts full of subdued excitement and relief that it was over successfully until the order came 'All hands on deck'. Leaving the wounded in charge of men, I got up on deck and saw on my way to the sick bay the *Nürnberg* in the grey light about 2,000 yards away her foremast shot away. Her conning tower shattered, in the midst of a furnace of flame. All around her the sea held swimming men. I went straight to the sick bay to find a shell had come through the deck above and filled the place with smoke and shell splinters and destroyed some bedding and the lights. The next half hour was ghastly, dressing bad burns and getting the wounded into cots. We were too busy attending to them to see anything of what was happening on deck. But on my way to fetch up some of the wounded below I looked for the *Dresden* and was just in time to see her masts going under. The sea was full of bobbing heads and faint cries were coming across the water. I heard after how our boats being riddled it took 20 minutes to patch them up before we could lower them and by steaming down into the survivors we got a few. But mostly they were too shocked to be able to catch the ropes we threw. The boats we sent out came back sinking, with 8 men. The intense cold of the water was too much for the swimmers almost at once. I was put in charge of the artificial respiration party on the aft deck and we worked with a will and brought round 8 or 9, the others were returned to the sea. Our casualties turned out to be eventually 5 killed (later on, several more died from shock), chiefly due to one unfortunate shell that caught A3 casemate and lit up our own ammunition there.

We had hot boiled ham, picnic fashion, and to bed except the watchkeepers and myself who kept the first watch. Spent it alternately on the Bridge with Dunn talking things over and in the sick bay attending to our wounded. To bed at 4 a.m. and slept *well*.

Next morning foggy. No idea where we are. Eventually met some whalers who piloted us into harbour 3 p.m. Our wireless house wrecked and so couldn't inform flag ship of our success. But we could hear them calling us up – *Kent, Kent* – and getting no answer they had sent out orders for a general search. So we arrived first at Port Stanley and the wireless there soon told the others of our safety. We watched them all struggle back to lick their wounds.

SEARCH AND CHASE

The next few days were far too busy – wounded, general repairing, and discussing with officers from other ships – to write this diary and I have never had the courage to attempt it since. We had 38 direct hits and innumerable splinter holes everywhere after the shells burst.

Friday December 18th. Weighed anchor at 3 a.m., entered the Straits of Magellan about 6. The tide with us swept us along at 16 knots, past lowish cliffs of alluvial character, very desolate with plenty of tussock grass and occasional herds of guanaco, a kind of llama. Plenty of lighthouses. The first narrows about 5 miles across we simply shot through. Patagonia stern and wild one side, Tierra del Fuego even more so the other, high rolling pampas. At 2 p.m. we anchored off Elizabeth Island and proceeded to coal from the *Trevanion*. At 7 we weighed again. A most weird sunset – deep maroon red bars. We passed Punta Arenas at midnight, a blaze of lights on the northern shore.

Saturday December 19th. At 6 a.m. waked to find ourselves in the narrow western straits – high snow mountains on both sides of the straits about 5 miles wide. Towards 11 the straits narrowed still more and the mountains became most interesting. Huge snow-fields, bits of glaciers and the scenery like a Norwegian fiord in winter. The wind bitterly cold and strong from the west. At midday huge snow range visible on Fuegian side.

The hills clothed by the waterside with luxuriant forests. Numerous little islands and inlets making a most wonderful scene. The sun shone out occasionally but only feebly. Mostly dull and cloudy on the highest summits. But still we were fortunate – they say they only get about six good days in the year here, and we have already had two of them. After lunch we sighted Mount Wharton a striking peak named after the father of our Torpedo Lieutenant Commander, who was a famous hydrographer and spent three years here charting the channels. Wharton Glacier ran down into the sea, a most imposing ice stream. We sighted several glaciers after this both sides and peaks running up to at least seven thousand feet if not more. One of the remarkable things about this part of the straits is the straightness of it. Dead straight for 50 miles or more and only a mile or two wide, it looked almost as if it had been cut by man. We anchored off Tamar Island at 7 p.m. and shortly after a visit by our Captain to the *Orama* we weighed again and put out through the widening straits to sea. We heard here that the Patagonia had interned one less enemy. No news of the *Dresden*. Hear that Whitby and Hartlepool have been bombarded by Germans.

Sunday December 20th. Proceeding north with one collier along the coast of Chile, rolling sea, misty and wet. Everyone more or less comfy. No news of *Dresden*.

Monday December 21st. Appreciably warmer. Sun shone out once and the sea calmer. Held survey on the damage to the crews kit during action. The Commander's overcoat when put on made us shriek with laughter. Full of holes as that of the raggedest tramp you ever saw. The shell that wrecked his cabin played havoc with his kit. I lost a bag damaged by salt water.

Tuesday December 22nd. Chased two vessels seen, one a whaler escaped inshore. The other a Chilean 'collier' turned out alright and proceeded to accompany us northward of her own free will. Something went wrong, however, with the wireless signals: the *Orama* read from us, 'We are chasing a cruiser,' instead of collier as it should have been. Result she rushed up at 19 knots ready for action and was very annoyed to find us looking at a tramp steamer.

Her Captain is senior to ours. Result, enquiries. The mountainous desolate shore plainly visible. We passed Cape Rapier light at midnight and are making for our secret base in the Chonos Islands this afternoon where we coal again! Albatrosses by the dozen following us ever since Magellan Straits.

Wednesday December 23rd. Arrived at ValleNar Roads yesterday 4 p.m.

We skirted the mountainous coast islands for some time, clothed with green forests and giving us peeps of huge mountains inland many of them snow covered. Passed Darwin Channel entrance and turned through a narrow entrance into a landlocked bay surrounded with islands all hilly and covered with green forests. Very pretty when the sun condescended to shine. Found the *Glasgow*, *Bristol*, *Orama*, and two colliers here. Today left port at daylight to patrol outside. Spent a great day chasing inoffensive Chilenos. Sea dead oily smooth with a huge swell. Held a *Kronikal* Committee.

Thursday December 24th. Christmas Eve! Came in to port 9 a.m. and proceeded to coal from *Pensilva*. Did a second coaling at 150 odd tons an hour. Some fun in the ward room after dinner including Waits from the crew forward who broke down badly however.

Friday December 25th. Christmas Day. Yesterday after coaling some of us tried to get ashore to get holly for decorations. A squall was blowing and although the officers double-banked the oars with the crew of the lifeboat we could make no headway against the wind and tide and ignominiously drifted to leeward. We were seen and rescued by the *Glasgow*'s steam boat which towed us back. Later on in the afternoon the C.P.O.s got there in calmer weather and brought back a boat load of arbutus, laurel, berberis, wild fuchsia trees and plenty of flowers, lilies, fuchsias and unknowns. So this morning we had a fuchsia tree at the top of each mast. Its red flowers made it look just like holly. The crew borrowed some of the officers' clothing and made up to represent us. They held a mock court martial which was great fun and imitated us beautifully. At 12 the Captain visited all the messes followed by the officers who had to taste the various plum puddings and other goodies. It was amazing to see what there still was in the ship in the way of extra food and how cheerful the men were in spite of no beer. In the ward room we had asked the warrant officers and the midshipmen to join us in some champagne before lunch. While there, a parcel arrived from 'the Mayor of Margate' for Dunn. It contained a set of infant's underclothing – Dunn being a bachelor. We hung the articles along the light rail above the table and they made an interesting decoration. The clothes arrived amongst the other things sent by the ladies of Kent apparently. After lunch the crew seized on every officer and carried him round the decks behind the funny party and a 'band'. Some officers went ashore in the afternoon. The P.M.O. being ill in bed with dysentery I stayed aboard. Very hard luck on Fleet Surgeon being ill at such a time. We did our best to cheer him up, however. After the return of the shore party laden with huge tree ferns, fuchsias, etc., we had a sing-song and some excellent new songs, one of which had escaped the lynx-eyed censor (the parson) and was much enjoyed, or at least two verses of it, 'Little by little, and bit by bit.' Our dinner in the evening was a triumph for the Paymaster and Cook. The decorations of ferns, fuchsia and lilies and baby's garments were really beautiful. Turtle soup. Pate de foie gras, turkey and salmon cutlets, and plenty of fizz and plum pudding. Afterwards the fun was kept up well. Jones' song (see the *Kent Kronikal*), and Burn's dancing being *the* features, especially the latter's last effort in an impromptu Salome costume. The Captain was our guest for the evening. We all remarked that it was the cheeriest Christmas on a ship we could remember and felt sorry for the sad folk (probably) at home.

Saturday December 26th. Got ashore in the afternoon for a picnic, about 15 of us. Landed in a little landlocked bay with beach and the forest running down to it. Perfect summer weather, blue sky and sea and high mountains all around us. Some of us plunged at once into the Virgin Forest over tree trunks, under creepers, up trees, along the tops of undergrowth, falling into deep mossy pits every few yards, picking flowers and digging up ferns. Jones climbed a tree and tore his pants badly. After a rest in a clearing on the hill side we struggled back to the beach to find the Marine Captain boiling water and opening tins of sausages. We all bathed and it was great to feel the water again all around one at once. It was quite warm. Then fried sausages, biscuits and cocoa – so good. After, we sketched, took photos and wandered. Only those who had been shut up in a ship for several months can appreciate properly how we enjoyed ourselves on shore again. The 'Major' was a fine chef and contributed largely to the success of the show.

Monday December 28th. *Glasgow* and *Bristol* went south and left us.

Tuesday December 29th. Left ValleNar Roads with *Orama* and two colliers, *Pensilva* and *Trevanion*, and proceeded north slowly. Sea rough and ship rolling 30–35 degrees each way.

Wednesday December 30th. Very rolly still. Have broken much crockery. I'm uncomfortable but I am not seasick nowadays.

Thursday December 31st. Left *Orama* last night and proceeding fast at 15 knots, put into Coronel alone this morning. The place is only a small coal-mining town near Concepcion. We got some fresh meat, fowls and fruit (cherries and plums), and fine fish.

This is a great treat for us. Also got the latest Chileno papers, and news of aeroplane raids on Cuxhaven. Learnt to our disgust that probably the mails we have been so eagerly looking forward to at Valparaiso, have gone south in the *Orita*. We were called up by this vessel by wireless but she got a panic that we must be a German cruiser and refused to give her position and the *Orama*'s Captain wouldn't take the trouble to find out whether the mails she said she was carrying for the Pacific Squadron included ours or not. She had 33 bags of it! Rejoined *Orama* at 5 o'clock and proceeding north again. 12 p.m. Have just had fine bowl of punch and *old lang syne* in ward room and heard 16 bells strike. (It only does this once a year.) What a momentous year for all of us.

Friday January 1st. Crawled north all day. *Orama* left us in the evening to go into Valparaiso.

Saturday January 2nd. Hung round Valparaiso all the afternoon about 10 miles outside, waiting for *Orama*. The atmosphere rather misty inland but occasionally able to catch glimpse of the Highest Andes. The lower hills of the coastline came first about 2,000–3,000 ft. Behind them 30 miles away rose bare dry peaks of 10,000–13,000 ft, and above them, towering above, the snow wreathed 20,000 footers. Aconcagua[9] I saw faintly several times as the sun set, thick with snow, 100 miles away.

Sunday January 3rd. *Orama* joined up this a.m. and signalled, 'Course N.18W.' That was all. No news. No word of our mails. As she was senior ship we couldn't ask. We all cursed her and her skipper. We do so want mails. Later on, however, she came closer and started to semaphore news. Mails hadn't been heard of. Had wired for them. *Formidable* sunk. Then a long list of promotions, including Wharton, our Torpedo Lieutenant Commander, to be Commander. Great rejoicings as he is a good fellow. He stood us fizz at lunch and we drank to his future career. Great fun in trying to provide him with a gold peaked hat (tin hat), and new stripes. Promotion being by selection and ordinarily due after 12 years, it becomes an anxious time about then for all in the service. If not promoted within 12–13 years, the chances are remote and they must retire at 45 as lieutenants, if they stay on as long which is rare. Wharton in peace time was certain for promotion, but there was the chance in war time that younger men who had seen active service might step up before him. Our action the other day helped him therefore. They have been promoting the 1st lieutenants of all ships in successful actions.

Published No. 2 of the *Kronikal*. It seemed to be appreciated. Especially picture competition and the presentation plate.

Monday January 4th. Put in to coal at Tongoy Bay. Stayed outside 3 miles limit and coaled from *Pensilva*. Perfect warm weather. Calm sea. Whales playing all round us. Some came so near us we threw coal on their shiny backs. They are a small kind but large beasts for all that, 50 feet long. Fished and caught what I thought must be a shark. Hauled it to the surface with difficulty and it turned out to be an octopus which dropped off at once. Shore looks brown and dry here, a lighthouse and the chimney of a copper smelting works – the only signs of civilization. Going

9   Aconcagua Mountain in Argentina.

tonight toward Cocquimbo where we may get our mails day after tomorrow.

Tuesday January 5th. At sea. *Orama* fired at a target towed by us and we fired at one towed by her.

Afternoon. Great excitement. Sighted suspicious vessel with collier close into coast, which dodged behind an island. Speed increased to 20 knots. Must be the *Prinz Eitel* an armed merchantman we want to meet. Vessel turned out to be the *Orama* which had left us in the morning to investigate something or other and which was now chasing a ship which turned out a British tramp.

Wednesday January 6th. Put into Cocquimbo – the old station for the British Squadron out here, but abandoned some years ago. The bay reminded me somewhat of Naples but the sea was yellow not blue. High mountains all around it and behind these the tops of snow peaks. La Serena on the north side of the bay and Cocquimbo round the corner to the south. The shore and beach very dry and rocky but inland up a valley where irrigation is carried on, much greener and trees in plenty.

Fired a salute as we came to anchor. Found two Chileno cruisers there and lots of sailing vessels. Leave limited to 4 officers. I stayed on board. Soon surrounded by boats. Chileno lieutenant called in *full* dress exactly like our English uniform to all intents, and looking very like an Englishman himself. In one of the boats we discovered and Englishman and a pretty Chilean lady in a canary jersey. Promptly invited beauty on board and she accepted. Englishman explained she couldn't speak a word of English!, and that they hoped to be married next month. We showed them the sights of the ship and the Commander showered bits of shell onto beauty, while the Commander (T) gave her a *Kent* hat ribbon which she promptly wore in her sailor hat. In the afternoon they returned with more beauty and a Mr Cargill – manager of a bank here and a big bug evidently. The old Wardroom was filled for tea. Got lots of fruit on board; pines, peaches, nectarines, figs, pears, bananas, cherries and flowers. The shore party returned full of beans. Hear our mail had arrived at Valparaiso.

Thursday January 7th. At sea, going N.W. towards St Felix.

Friday January 8th. Still steaming N.W.

Saturday January 9th. At daybreak rushed up at full speed to the Islands of St Felix in case the Germans were using it as a secret base. Found no-one there and a poor anchorage on the west, exposed to the Pacific swell. The Island of St Felix, off which we were, gave no promise of being able to land. The surf was breaking in huge clouds of spray on precipitous rocks. We were disappointed as we had hoped to be able to do a bit of Robinson Crusoe life on the island and make it one of our bases. Opposite the island was a jagged pinnacled rock about 400 ft high very picturesque and called Peterborough Cathedral on account of its resemblance to that place. We anchored between it and the main island. Being anxious to see the effect of a lyddite shell exploding and to know whether it would explode without a fuse we obtained permission to fire one shell at the cathedral rock. Officers and crew watched the experiment with breathless interest. All eyes glued to glasses and then at last the boom of the gun. We watched the huge cliffs of the rock for several exciting seconds and then an amazed roar broke out from us all. The shot had fallen into the sea half way there. Explanation being that half a charge was used and someone forgot to alter the sights which were for full charges. Guns got his leg well pulled for days about it. Fishing was very popular. Forward they kept catching any amount of fish. Soon the officers all joined in. The Commander catching several immediately, I couldn't get a bite. Bilben, the chief sick bay steward, caught 20 out of the sick bay porthole. Chiefly mullet, bream and rock fish. In the afternoon we manned 3 boats and set off to explore the coast and to blow up fish. Our boat – ahead of the others got in quite close and right up under the huge cliffs and into a cave. It was crawling with black, loathsome looking crabs. The cliffs were very interesting; formed by perfectly-well-defined layers of lava and ashes alternately, laid horizontally. The ash layers had weathered away leaving ledges of lava on which were the nests and eggs of countless sooty terns. We blew up five charges of gun cotton, but only got four or five big black rock fish.

Both the exercise and change made us all feel better. Left the same evening for Peru, passing one of the islands said to be quite inaccessible owing to its sides being perpendicular smooth rock. It must have been several miles long and about 2,000–3,000 ft high. Still rolling.

Sunday January 10th. At sea. Warmer, swell lessening.

Monday January 11th. Still heaving. Danckwerts birthday.

Tuesday January 12th. Coaled at sea. The swell less, but still quite enough. We managed quite well, however, the first time we have done this without any shelter. Wrote letters. *Orama* thought she detected German wireless about so we made for the coast.

Wednesday January 13th. Explored Independencia Bay and San Nicholas Bay but found nothing there. The coast extraordinarily dry and barren, sandy drifts right up, thousands of feet up the mountain's sides. Occasional peeps of snow peaks in behind.

Thursday January 14th. Travelling north near the coast, *Orama* has gone to Callao with our mails this evening.

Friday January 15th. Sports finals. These were rather interesting. The tug of war was won by the petty officers after a fine tug with the foretopmen. The officers (we), had previously lost to the petty officers after a thrilling tug. The hundred yards open race came to a dead heat between Gunlayer Jenkins and Midshipman Liley. Potato race very amusing, also sack and the obstacle race too. The prizes were given away by the Duchess of Vallemar, as played by Lieutenant Jones R.N.R. His get up was wonderfully good, and his speech to the prize winners something to laugh at for days. Towards the end a signal boy came up for his prize who often keeps watch with Jones on the Bridge at night. Turning to him with a beaming smile the Duchess said, 'There is no need for me to say anything to *you*. We have spent so many nights together.' The crew shrieked with laughter while the boy tried to hide his blushes behind his prize, a tin of sardines and another of pineapples.

All this time we were cruising off Callao, and we looked into Ancon Bay. Here we passed a rocky islet covered with sealions making a fearful row. Opposite it was a guano-covered island with people digging at the stuff on top. Ancon itself was a little patch of trees in Sahara of sand – huge mountains rising up behind. We watched a little train start out and lose itself in the desert on its way to Lima.

Saturday/Sunday January 16/17th. Sailed south to San Nicholas Bay. Had a little excitement chasing a ship that turned out to be the *Orama*.

Monday January 18th. Took colliers into San Nicholas Bay, where we found the *Orama* anchored. After waiting there until the afternoon we came out on patrol while she coaled. Caught two eels, my first catches. Ironic congratulations from everyone. The bay is uninhabited and a sandy waste of mountains sloping back gently. Saw some Indians with horses on the shore and their trail over the hills.

Tuesday January 19th. My birthday. A most interesting day. Redhead had fixed up a boom and a fishing tackle which projected over the side and towed a bit of white rag clear of the ship's wake. It was so arranged that when the fish hooked himself the extra strain caused the boom to tip and become vertical. This gave notice to everyone near and we would all rush to the line. It is intended to fix up an electrical contact so that a bell is rung when we catch a fish. We tried it for the first time properly this morning and caught three bonita. The first weighed 27½ lb, the other two about 15 lb. Great excitement on deck before breakfast especially amongst the Scottish fishermen who form so large a part of our R.N.R. crew.

Later on we stopped the P.S.N.Co. S.S. *Ortega*, the ship that brought us our first mails and whose Captain had given us so much fresh fruit etc., at Abrolhos. He had also escaped the *Dresden* by running up an uncharted channel in Smyth's Sound when she hove alongside one day and told him to surrender. Redhead brought back any amount of fresh fruit and also sodawater and a splendid huge iced cake with H.M.S. *Kent* on it in fresh icing. This was voted to be my birthday cake and very good it was too.

The crew of *Ortega* serenaded us as before. Later in the day we stopped the P.S.N.Co.s S.S. *Orissa*. The *Ortega* was going north

41

home *via* Panama; the *Orissa* south *via* the straits. We met a Japanese collier and also a mineral ore ship with 6 or 7 derricks and no proper masts. In section she was like the sketch and was originally built to evade the Suez Canal dues (the width being measured across the deck and not at the water line).

Dinner was remarkable for fresh vegetables and fruit, and we enjoyed the fresh newspapers after, too.

Wednesday January 20th. Anchored at San Nicholas Bay and coaled. No fish. Left evening for Callao.

Thursday January 21st. At sea.

Friday January 22nd. Arrived Callao. A fine bay dotted with pretty fishing boats carrying a lot of sail. The usual sandy-looking mountains everywhere. Harbour stiff with German merchantmen and sailing ships. We made the air hideous with salutes. The Peruvian Navy represented by three quaint-looking gunboats, and two up-to-date French submersibles replied but neglected the courtesy of flying our flag. The orders were that officers might go ashore but only in plain clothes, and only a third at a time. I got the whole day as Burn and P.M.O. wouldn't go. Half of us had not got complete sets of mufti, and so when the second boat got to the pier the first party undressed and provided the next with clothes. This was done more or less privately in the picket boat's cabin.

Callao is a dusty place given over to shipping. Everyone of importance lives at Lima eight miles away up a valley and visible from Callao in this clear atmosphere. It never rains and the roofs are flat and without gutters. I sought a dentist and found a dapper little Peruvian named Eduardo who stopped eight holes and charged me £3.15/– [£3.75]. Very neat and gentle he was too. We talked French. The Captain came to him in the middle of my ordeal and he did something for him too. I bought some shoes from a Chinese shop for 6/– [30p] and various odds and ends. Everything very dear. Had lunch at the Club. Two Englishmen named MacIver and Johnson looked after me like brothers. I invited them off to the ship for tea in return. Johnson has a brother at Clifton College in Rintouls House. Must look him up on return. Owing to dentist hadn't time to get to Lima. Returned to ship for tea with the visitors, about 15 ladies and a dozen men.

Burn discovered a kind of cousinship with one jolly girl. A Mrs Wingfield knew the Captain when he was midshipman out there before. A Mrs Ashton lived in Clifton during her time home and Hedly Hill confined her. Redhead had been up to Lima all day to see his brother-in-law. He returned with friends from Lima. They stayed to dinner. The resulting jovial evening will not be forgotten by seven inhabitants of Lima in a hurry. They simply loaded the Mess with presents of fresh fruit: mangoes, prickly pears, avocado pears, limes, quinces, grapes, bananas, pineapples, oranges, lettuces, chillies, etc. Howard very amusing towards midnight. Burns' Salome dance the best he has ever done. Heard when the *Orama* came in a week ago all the Germans ashore took her to be the *Prinz Eitel Friedrich* and came out in boats to meet her and dressed the ships in harbour. Their disgust when they came alongside and saw the name on the ship's side was very humorous – for the English.

Saturday January 23rd. At sea going south.

Sunday January 24th. At sea going south.

Monday January 25th. We are trying to call up the *Newcastle* by wireless, apparently she ought to be with us according to orders received at Callao.

Tuesday January 26th. Coaled at sea in spite of a fairly obvious swell, by going ahead into it at 2 knots all the time. The *Travanion*'s officers fishing for drinks, poor souls, as they don't get anything aboard their own hull.

Wednesday January 27th. Have got into touch with *Newcastle*, who is to meet us off Antofagasta on Friday. *Orama* gone into Mollendo for news. Heard by wireless of a fight between battle cruisers in the North Sea and that *Blucher* is sunk. Had night action rehearsal after chasing an oil ship with her lights out. Saw Iquique and many sailing vessels anchored about 10 miles away.

Thursday January 28th. Stopped engines all day. I floated out a bait on some bit of wood to *windward* and to my own amazement caught a fine dolphin of 9 lb. It was all the colours of the rainbow in the water. Captain photographed me with it. Soon after caught another larger one, but as I was hauling it up the ship's side it broke the wire and escaped. Yet another Tilling let off the hook as he was taking it over railing. Cooked for dinner, it gave us the best bit of fish we have had this commission, very tender and delicious. The Captain was quite enthusiastic over its flavour. The dolphin is *not* a porpoise, although often confounded with the latter. The sun very warm and the back of my neck very sore after exposure to the afternoon sun while fishing. Have rigged up miniature rifle range for practice in afternoons. Driven all our captive golf balls overboard yesterday afternoon.

Hear that our Valparaiso mail is on board the S.S. *Peru*, and we are looking out eagerly for her as she comes north.

Friday January 29th. Captain sent me a message this morning to say that there would be an opportunity for me to fish for half an hour as he was going to stop the ship. Evidently he enjoyed that dolphin! *Orama* rejoined us this afternoon after a visit to Iquique. At 4 o'clock the *Newcastle*, the *Celtic* of the White Star Line, and a collier steamed up from the south. Not a flag or signal of any sort did they show for some time and then only a curt message for us to stay out and patrol while they went into a bay north of Antofagasta. Later on *Orama* signalled that she had discovered that the *Celtic* had mails for us. We asked when we should be able to get mails and no notice was taken of our signal. The *Celtic* looked huge – four masts and two funnels – 21,000 tons as against the 11,000 tons of the *Orama* and the *Orama* looks huge to us. The *Celtic* has come out specially with mails and stores for us. After dinner the signal has come. Proceed S.S.W. We are going to a bay tomorrow morning, Blanco-something or other with the *Celtic*, *Orama*, and two colliers. The *Newcastle* has gone north to Mexico. Why she couldn't have arranged for us to fetch off our mails at once I don't know. It could have been done so easily. The ways of the navy executive when he gets to 4-stripe rank are weird. Captains seem to hate each other, and love to snub the junior ones of their rank seemingly.

Saturday January 30th. Arrived at Blanco Encalada early and anchored close in shore with the *Celtic* and *Orama*. This place is rather interesting for Chile. High mountains rise up directly from the water's edge to about 2,000–3,000 ft. Directly opposite is a gorge leading up into the midst of higher mountains behind whose tops we can see – wonderful peaks all red and green and purple from some mineral or other. A road from the beach runs up this gorge to an old mine well engineered and hugging the precipices. The surf on the shore makes a continual roar, echoed back by the hills. We found a party of fishermen encamped on the shore – they were dependent for their water on a distilling plant. They visited the place each summer from Antofagasta. We made them our friends by giving them coal, oil and fresh meat. There is no water or any living thing on shore except a few cacti on the summits of the hills where the clouds come down at night.

Immediately we anchored, boats put off to the *Celtic* and soon returned with 89 bags of mails. How we revelled in our letters and parcels and newspapers. But not for long. All day and all night we have been taking in fresh stores, every possible conceivable thing: wheelbarrows, glasses, brushes, boots, bales of cloth, timber, ropes, food by the ton, ammunition; engineers' spares and fittings by the ton too. The noise all night outside my cabin, as they shot the cases of condensed milk down the ladder, would have kept anyone except a naval man awake. Boats buzzed back and forward between the ships continually day and night. The *Celtic* is a huge ship. She is alleged to have left England with 17,000 tons of stores on board valued at about 5 millions. She has supplied two or three dozen ships already and still holds plenty more. A thousand carcases of beef and mutton, a thousand fish were taken on board her at Liverpool. She is the largest store ship that has ever been sent out, and yet by the side of the *Mauretania* or the *Aquitania* especially she would look quite dwarfed.

Our mail is dated from England on dates from Nov 22nd to Dec 8th. The mails of Nov 6th–22nd are on the *Peru* which sailed from Valparaiso on 27th of January, and which we may meet on her way north in a day or two.

Completed tonight my week as mess president.

Sunday January 31st. Taking in stores all day up to 10 p.m. I visited the *Celtic* taking over three sick men to send them home. One is Private Salter, R.M.L.I., a motor-bus driver in Bristol who lives at Fishponds somewhere. He has rheumatism. The *Celtic* is huge; our own little quarter-deck seemed a prison after their spacious promenades. At dinner P.M.O. provided us with an immense plum pudding which had come out in the mails. Very good. After dinner put to sea for patrol. The decks littered with unpacked casks, cases etc. Have received an addition to the Mess in Lieutenant Skinner, who has been sent out to take Rayner's place. As the sun set tonight the alpen glow on the distant peaks was as fine as I have ever seen it, glowing, alive, ruby coloured. Made me long for Switzerland again.

Monday February 1st. Came in early and anchored again. Went ashore for the morning and visited the remains of the old camp. Everything being so dry was well preserved. Find the bleached skeleton of a man, many whale bones and all the litter of a town, broken bottles, etc. No water anywhere. Close by the landing stage some Chilenos had occupied an old wooden shanty, fitted up a distilling plant for water, and spent their time fishing and drying the fish in the sun. They were the only people there. Sand everywhere. I found some fine pieces of copper ore evidently brought down from the mine inland, now no longer worked apparently.

In the afternoon fished for rock fish and caught two ugly red brutes about 2 lb, but good eating. Went out to patrol at night.

Tuesday February 2nd. Came in to pick up our boats and then sailed south with the *Kent*.

Wednesday February 3rd. At sea. General Quarters.

Thursday February 4th. I fished all day with floating bait – about 200 yards away from the ship – but didn't have a bite all day. Dolphins must like warmer *water*, although the air is hot enough here. Took in 800 tons and pounded north for a few hours at night to pick up a new collier, the *Braunton*. Then south again. *Orama* meanwhile puts into Cocquimbo.

Friday February 5th. Published the 3rd No. of the *Kronikal*. *Celtic* has gone to Valparaiso and will fetch our mails.

Sunday February 7th. *Celtic* rejoined and proceeded south with us. No signal or news so we were forced to content ourselves with looking at her and realizing our mails were in her. The sea quite moderately calm too. However, after tea I woke up to find the ship stopped and saw our boat going away for the mails. Received about 30 letters from Nov 12th to Dec 30th. The ward soon, as usual, a great sight littered with papers and a few Christmas cards.

Monday/Tuesday February 8/9th. Steaming south to ValleNar Roads.

Wednesday February 10th. Sea rolling, but not badly.

Thursday February 11th. Arrived ValleNar again. Weather perfect – slightly cold in the wind perhaps. Anchored and *Orama* proceeded to coal. Three day job for her.

Friday February 12th. Stayed on board all day. Others went for a picnic to beach. We landed an observation party who camped on a high hill overlooking sea. Fished with no success. Weather perfect and the mornings with mist rising round the peaks reminded one of a Pacific lagoon. Boats crews practised pulling for regatta; divers dove, and engineers cleaned or did something to the engines. All busy.

Saturday February 13th. Ship has a very holiday air. In the morning went out in the picket boat with Commander Wharton and two torpedoes which we practised dropping from the dropping gear. Great fun playing round with these. One refused to proceed after being dropped. Result – opportunity for me to have a look inside him. The chasing after them at full speed and recovering quite good fun. In the afternoon went ashore with Redhead and Wharton for a walk. We broke through the fringe of forest and climbed up on to the hill top of Three Finger Island. Even up there very rough going through scrub and bog. The view marvellous. Blue calm lagoon. *Kent* quite smart in new grey paint, and green mountainous islands all round up to 5,000 or 6,000 ft. Snow in distance on higher Andes of mainland. *Kent* looked like a little toy on a blue mirror.

Sunday February 14th. Went ashore in the afternoon with the snotties. Broke through forest again with Wright and Ross and made our way across island to a fiord-like bay I had seen the day previous. Trying to get through the forest the other side, down to the water, proved impossible at last, and so had to return. Bush simply impenetrable. Feet-deep holes, moss and tree trunks and shrub. So returned and after a council of war tried a fresh place and got through very hot onto a lovely beach at the end of a fiord a mile or more long. Bathed and returned by same tracks to landing beach where the other snotties had hot coffee and salmon waiting for us. After tea explored more forest and beach and found a cliff covered with a scarlet leaved aloe, very gorgeous.

(The pig Dennis was landed on Friday. He revelled in the sand and ploughed it up with his nose. Didn't care for the forest and felt lonely if left and rushed back to his friend the Butcher and fed on tinned sausages!) In the evening made a huge bonfire and sat round it till the steam boat came to take us back.

Monday February 15th. Coaled. I fished. Discovered shark-like fish about 3–4 ft long, which kept sucking at the bait but couldn't hook them firmly. Very tantalising. Octopus and cuttle fish plantiful. *Braunton* our new collier worked 5 holds!

Tuesday February 16th. Regatta over a course 2 miles long against the *Orama* boats. We won 5 out of 7 races. Officers won theirs (one mile) by two seconds, after strenuous race. Everyone enjoyed the sport. In afternoon I discovered smoke on island and later boats with a hunting party came alongside. They had dogs, and numerous skins of seal, vicuna etc. We gave them fresh bread and tobacco and sugar and they gave us a tiny otter for a pet. Otter died next day, from a surfeit of sardines! The ship very interested in the Chilean hunters. Very simple things amuse us now after so much monotony. But we are sorry our secret uninhabited island base has been discovered. Weather still gorgeous. Ship renovated and ship's crews all the better for a run ashore.

Wednesday/Thursday/Friday February 17/18/19th. At sea. Rolling dreadfully going north. *Orama* gone to Valparaiso for mails. We going to Coronel. Much crockery broken and meals an ordeal. Not sea-sick glad to say.

Saturday February 20th. Anchored under lee of Santa Maria Island off Coronel and coaled 300 tons. Put into Coronel in afternoon. Shore party went off in mufti and returned hilarious with Messrs Clark and Loveday, two Englishmen. Clark very young-looking, typical clean Englishman just married yet going home to get a commission. Loveday thin and ill after nine month gastric ulcer. Had a hilarious evening in spite of Padre's absence from the piano. He has gone to Valparaiso in *Orama* to get a new upper set of teeth. Had mouth organs and a *Fahtoon*. Ended up with a rugby scrum. Devon versus Scotland and many bruises.

Fruit plentiful: pears, apples, plums, nectarines. Everyone bought plenty, Bum boats did roaring trade.

Sunday February 21st. Redhead, Wharton and I up early and got ashore at 7.30 for a long walk along the coast and then up into the hills, through lovely forests of fir and eucalyptus. Geranium hedges a fine sight. Numerous coal mines along the sea shore. Cut down onto a white sandy beach at last and bathed in the surf. Cold but enjoyable, walked back by the railway line. Visitors to lunch aboard. In the afternoon put to sea and met *Orama* at Santa Maria Island. Long confab between the two Captains. Steamed *north* all night. This in spite of fact we were destined for the south to search Smyth Sound for *Dresden*. Mails.

Monday February 22nd. Steaming south again for Coronel. Appears the *Orama*'s Captain had sent a wire home at Valparaiso asking if he need be separated from the *Kent* as ordered. He had been ordered to go north and search for *Eitel Friedrich*: we to go south to Smyth Sound to search for *Dresden*. The answer was to be sent to Coronel. Put in there in the afternoon much to everyone's surprise. Telegram orders us both south. *Orama* to be the bum boat of the fleet and fetch stores, etc., to Punta Arenas for fleet. We to join *Bristol* and *Glasgow* and search Last Hope Inlet and the Beagle Channel.

Tuesday/Wednesday February 23/24th. At sea. Fine weather. No rolling. Overhauled the *Elm Branch* after a race. Captain tells me we are going into Smyth Sound *via* the Trinidad Inlet and to anchor tomorrow at Alert Bay where there are plenty of fish. So we are to run the seine net. Looking forward to seeing these magnificent fiords. Speed *15 knots*!

Thursday February 25th. All plans altered again. Wireless informs us that *Glasgow* has search Last Hope Inlet and found nothing. We are now to go to Port Tamar in the straits and coal there.

Friday February 26th. Entered Magellan Straits early this morning. Near Port Tamar where we were to anchor I was in the conning tower watching for an alleged ship when I noticed the ship alter course 8 points to port and swinging round in a big curve, make up north again through a channel which I soon discovered to my delight to be Smyth Sound.

Plans all altered again in the night by wireless. Apparently the *Dresden* had been seen in Last Hope. The *Bristol* and *Glasgow* were there already waiting for us to join them. Hopes of an action ran high. Smyth's Sound and Last Hope Inlet take a lot of describing. The channel varies from a mile or two in places to a few hundred yards only. Tiny islands, tree covered, fill the larger channels. Huge bare granite, and lava and limestone mountains rise from the water's edge where a thick undergrowth covers them, up through scraggy forest to bare glacier-worn rock. In places, for instance near the Kirk Narrows, entrance to Last Hope, several huge glaciers come almost down to sea level. Every now and then distant peeps of snowfields, glaciers and huge peaks. It's a land of mist and rain and dreaminess: only when the sun shines it makes a wonderful picture. We met the *Bristol* anchored off Last Hope and left her with her collier. Her rudder broke inside and she had come through the narrows without – a great feat. We pushed on at 16 knots! and had just got under the glaciers near Kirk Narrows when news came that *Glasgow* was returning. She said she was sure now she had been chasing herself – that the rumours of a vessel having been seen referred to herself and not the *Dresden*. I was very disappointed at not going further into this fascinating inland sea.

Returned to *Bristol*'s anchorage in Smyth Sound with *Glasgow*. Several photos of glacier. Natives alongside.

Saturday February 27th. *Bristol* returned home for repairs. *Glasgow* coals. I fish. Party goes ashore and returns with buckets of mussels for dinner, very good scalloped. In the afternoon persuaded the Pilot and Shorty to join in a walk. Land 4 p.m. on mainland and fight our way through the thickest bush ever seen yet, beats ValleNar even, and much of it holly. A continuous steep climb over boggy ground and rock brought us at 6 p.m. to the summit of the hill about 2,300 ft. Weather cloudy but what view we had, magnificent islands, mountains, lakes and channels, and to the west a flat plain even, enclosed by hills. The high peaks all hidden by cloud. The *Bristol* and *Glasgow* little toy ships below. We fell rather than walked down in 35 minutes. Saw the droppings of vicuna and flushed a covey of ?snipe (whistly birds, about size of blackbird – grey). Thoroughly enjoyed the walk. The Pilot and Scotsman thoroughly at home on hills and too fast to follow comfortably. But I got to top first after all by taking things steadily even if more slowly.

The natives here very interesting. Came out to us in a crazy canoe. Three men, three women and four children. The children naked. Temperature like an English winter. The men and women wore some cast-off seamen outer clothes, not buttoned up. Very low types. The baby of 3 smoked a cigarette when we threw them some and eagerly took all the bread and refuse we gave them. Heard dogs barking at night in their camp which is too far off to visit, unfortunately.

We have commissioned the picket boat as H.M.S. *Gillingham*. She is a steamboat, with half cabin after, and a foc's'le, of about 12 tons. Have put in a wireless mast and apparatus, maxim gun, and she is to take two torpedoes and a crew of 13 men. Commander, Wharton, gunner and a midshipman (Burridge). Her improvised mast makes her look a most natty little vessel. Her wireless worked today at 8 miles distance over a mountain. She is to explore the channels down south where we hear now the *Dresden* is. It is alleged that the *Dresden*'s officers have been taking week-ends at Punta Arenas! Her crew expect to be away for several days at a time. Cold and uncomfortable, but I wish I could go too.

Sunday February 28th. Coaled until 2.30, averaging 212 tons, easily our record. Took in 1,000 tons too. The *Cairnross* a fine collier, new with *geared turbines*. Went down and saw the gearing, which is two rows of helical gearing, drip feed to contacts and very quiet. Proceeded south at 3.30. Squally weather. The night very violent wind in the Magellan Straits.

Monday March 1st. Picked up *Bristol* in Fortescue Bay. The picket boat left us 8 a.m. looking very business-like and went to *Bristol* who stayed there. We proceeded slowly east, through the straits and then down south through the Magdalen Channel to Sholl Bay, where we anchored and found the *Glasgow*. The Magdalen Sound very grand. Glaciers every mile on either side. S.E. of Sholl Bay is Mount Sarmiento, easily the highest mountain I have seen so far here in Fuego, alleged to be 7,300 ft, but it looks 10,000 ft. The real peak rises from a huge massif, covered with snow and from it several huge glaciers descend. The largest, a magnificent stream of ice, some 2 miles across near its end, curves round in a fine sweep south and pokes its nose right out into the sea, making a beach of the terminal moraine. Owing to the clouds I could only catch an occasional glimpse of the peak and can't describe the shape as I should like. But the whole region here reminds one of the Zermatt Valley filled up to the level of the Riffel Alp with water. Peaks all round jagged and very steep *à la* Gabelhorn or Matterhorn, with the huge snowfield and massif of the Sarmiento range to correspond with Monte Rosa group.

Our plan of operations was to sweep the Barbara Channel and in particular Icy Sound where *Dresden* is alleged to be. Had arranged for a tug to meet us at Sholl Bay from Punta Arenas to help in the search, the tug to go up the small bays. No tug there, however. Anchored for night.

Tuesday March 2nd. Returned to Fortescue Bay and picked up our picket boat and returned to Sholl Bay and anchored for night.

Plan of Operations. *Bristol* and *Orama* to block the two northern entrances to Barbara Channel. *Glasgow* to search slowly helped by tug and picket boat while *Kent* dashed up and stopped Gonzales Channel bolt hole. The tug joined us early on.

Wednesday March 3rd. He is to have £3,000 if he discovers the *Dresden* and £60 a day for searching! Up anchor at daybreak. I got up early to study Sarmiento, and was well rewarded for 2 hours very cold vigil on the quarter-deck. Magnificent peak (in clouds) but glaciers very fine. Proceeded down Cockburn Channel in and out of islands, glaciers all around and peaks galore. The weather *fine* and *sunny*. Great luck as the Barbara is unsurveyed. After breakfast, and as we entered the Barbara Channel, it was one long panorama of wooded islands and peaks behind. No snow to speak of in its southern portion. The channels in places extremely narrow and often we could have thrown a stone on to the land on either side. One place kelp (?a rock) almost touched the side. The picket boat and the tug and *Glasgow* came on behind searching the innumerable coves, inlets, and behind the islands.

About 4 p.m. got off Gonzales and still kept on slowly about 5 knots past Bedford Bay which was named by and after the grandfather of our Commander. The *Glasgow* had passed us by now and led us into snow fiords again until about 6 p.m. we got off Brodrip Bay and opposite Icy Sound. All day we had been cleared for action, crews at their guns, ready round any headland to find our foe. The excitement as we neared Icy Sound was intense. Our picket boat rejoined us about 6.30 and was told to go ahead and search the sound. Meanwhile we watched the imposing scenery; high mountains with fine glaciers around us for ¾ of a circle and opening out of it, at the head, a deep narrow inlet closed in at the top by the most imposing glacier most of us on board had ever seen. A solid wall of ice a mile across and about 700–1,000 ft high, very steep and dropping off lumps of ice into the water which floated off as little icebergs. The sound was 6 miles long, and it was dark when Wharton returned with the disappointing news that NO *Dresden* was to be found. Slept well after 16 hours of watching scenery, grateful that the weather had been so sunny.

Thursday March 4th. Anchored until 8 a.m. in Brodrip Bay. Although weather was so sunny yesterday the wind that came suddenly in squalls off the ice fields were very violent and cold. We called them wullywahs. One such cyclone broke the *Bristol*'s fore topgallant mast. The wullywahs off Icy Glacier last night were very bad. Today have had orders from Admiralty to go to neighbourhood of Juan Fernandez where a collier is alleged to be going to meet the *Dresden* on March 5th. The *Bristol* to go home and the *Glasgow* and *Orama* to search Last Hope Inlet again. So we are going 17 knots west through the straits again. Hope to catch her coaling possibly but we are two days late. To get out of Barbara Sound into straits we came through Shag Narrows only 100 yards across, quite a gorge, and true to its name, full of flying shag. Could have tossed a pebble onto the shore one side. Shot through *with* 8 knot tide at about 20 knots! against millions of shag coming opposite way. Most alarming.

Friday/Saturday March 5/6th. Racing N.N.W. at 17 knots through gorgeously fine calm sea. My cabin vibrates at this speed but not enough to worry. The rendezvous is at 37S.80W. Fourteen albatrosses following, keeping up with hardly ever a flap of their huge wings. Wonder if we shall catch the *Dresden* at last, our only chance is to get the collier first and for the *Dresden* to arrive without any coal left. Spent 4 hours in engine room with Foreman. Very interesting.

Sunday March 7th. Arrived day break at rendezvous 80W.37S. Nothing there. Weather dull. Waiting round for them to turn up. Our trouble is we are getting short of coal. Can't wait beyond Tuesday night then must push back to Coronel and order coal from Valparaiso. Wish we had *Glasgow* with us. I fished in the afternoon but no luck.

Monday March 8th. P.M.O. insists that as today is just 3 months to the day since the Battle something will happen. Much fun this a.m. The Marines turn out and fire volleys at a target on the sea with rifles and maxim. Dreadful noise but it doesn't seem to frighten away a young shark which flags round the ship. I rush down on the news and get a cod line and with only a cod hook and some pork, fish for him. Am jeered at by several who say, '*that* will never hold him'. At last, tired of chasing round the ship after the beast I leave the line floating out over the stern, and when I return just catch a young seven-foot shark going for the bait. Hook him firmly and then begins intense excitement. Have to play shark tenderly as I only have the hook on three strands of fine wire. He

.... Class cruiser, at anchor off Canada in 1915.

The author aboard the Kent, *on which he was to serve for 28 months before returning home* (left).

Food was often in short supply and Captain Allen of the Kent *encouraged his junior officers to fish. It not only kept up their morale, it also helped provision the ship* (bottom).

A shark is landed, watched by some of the crew (top).

The Butcher and pig Dennis have an afternoon nap (left).

Dennis, as drawn by the author. The crew became so fond of their pig that they refused to eat him, so Dennis was swopped for a turtle with a Japanese ship off Mexico (bottom).

The Silk Ensign of H.M.S. Kent *photographed as the Battle of the Falklands was beginning* (left).

A sketch of the Kent, *taken from the front page of the* Kent Kronikal *which was edited by T.B. Dixon and published by him in an edition of 5* *copies* (bottom).

The officers' heads (lavatories) were severely damaged by shell fire during the Falklands Action (right).

The ship's crew crowd round a shell hole in the ventilator to the stokehold (bottom left).

Sergeant Mayes, hero of H.M.S. Kent, standing next to the damaged ventilator (bottom right).

The Leipzig hidden by smoke. Photograph taken from the fore-top of the Kent *during the battle*

Short of coal and desperate for extra speed, the crew hacked up the targets and stripped the cabins of wooden fittings to feed the furnace

T.B. Dixon in later life, when he had attained the rank of Surgeon Captain (inset).

The Falkland Islands Battle Memorial 'In Commemoration of the Battle of the Falklands, In which the British Squadron . . . under the command of Vice-Admiral F.C. Doveton Sturdee K.C.B., C.V.O., destroyed the German Squadron under Vice-Admiral Graf Von Spee, Thereby saving the colony from capture by the enemy' (top right).

Snowballing on South Georgia (bottom right).

ashore took her to be the Prinz Eitel Frederick & came out in boats to meet her & dressed the ships in harbour. Their disgust when they came alongside & saw the name on the ship side was very humerous – for the English.

Sat. Jan 23.   at sea foggy South
Sunday Jan 24   at Sea foggy South
Monday Jan 25   We are trying to call up the Newcastle by wireless apparently she ought to be with us according to orders received at Callao.

Tuesday. Jan 26. Coaled at sea in spite of a fairly obvious swell. by going ahead into it at 2 knots all the time. The Trevannions officers fishing for drinks poor souls as they don't get anything aboard their own hulk.

Wednesday Jan 27. Have got into touch with Newcastle. who is to meet us off Antofogasta on Friday. Orama gone into Mollendo for News. Heard by wireless of a fight between battle cruisers in the North Sea & that Blucher is sunk. Had night action rehearsal after chasing an oil ship with her lights out Saw Iquique and many sailing vessels anchored about 10 miles away

A page taken from the diary.

dived repeatedly, but steadily pressure brings him up time and again. Meanwhile about a hundred people are crowded round shouting out advice and trying to take the line. Then the Commander arrives with his Mauser pistol and puts several shots into him when he comes to the surface: my fear all the time being that the bullets may cut the line. Gradually I worked him forward, towards the cutter alongside which is scraping the ship's side. Then a rope with a noose is passed down by line and the cutter's crew put it over his head. While doing this, the shark dives and nearly fouls the propeller and gets free. Finally, the noose is drawn tight and he is hoisted onto the quarter-deck, where he kicks and turns and snaps and bleeds from his bullet wounds. Someone cuts his spine across near the tail and I have caught my first shark. Seven foot long about 140 lb. A young one. Secure his spine for a walking stick. This is said to augur great good luck. Arrange with cook for shark-fin soup tonight. In the afternoon discover another shark and just going to hook him when Commander shoots him with service revolver. He floats away to die. I very annoyed because he wouldn't allow me the sport of hooking him. I was fishing over the stern at about 3.20 p.m. when the propellers began to revolve unexpectedly. Then a boy rushes onto quarter-deck to say three-funnelled cruiser on the starboard bow! The *Dresden* at last. I hauled in my line and then ran for my glasses and to tell the P.M.O. asleep in his cabin.

A slight fog had hung around all day and, suddenly lifting at 3.20, disclosed the *Dresden* 11,000 yards away, stopping. She was too amazed to run away apparently at once. She looked huge – very light, high up out of the water – therefore must be short of coal. Looked so large in the mist that most people felt incredulous at first and thought she must be a Chilean ship. However, as we run up our ensign she turned tail and fled to the westward, N.88W. approx. Her wireless began to buzz and we started to 'jam' it but she had got three words through before we got the tune. The excitement on board may be imagined. Decks soon cleared and all extra woodwork chopped up, including the great target (Pat 6) much to Commander's joy who hates hoisting it in and out. We rather slow in getting up speed but work up gradually to 160 revolutions (even more than at the Falklands). But in about an hour *Dresden* increases the range from 17,000 to 20,000 yards. She has a list to starboard but it doesn't seem to stop her speed which must be about 24–25 knots. Then she slows down to our speed and keeps 20,000 yards ahead. It looks a hopeless chase but anything may happen yet. She may burst a boiler. At 4.30 everyone is ordered aft to sit over the propeller and make it 'bite'. No good. Not gaining. The old *Kent* is responding nobly. The Wardroom is almost shaken to pieces with the terrific vibration. All hands have tea. There is a strong south wind and slightly choppy sea and we hurtle through it with spray coming over the fo'c'sle. Everyone very cheerful and grinning. The band plays on the quarter-deck to the crew squatting there and couples soon start dancing. At 6.30 it is seen we can't expect to catch her unless she has an accident. At seven we have dinner as usual. At eight it getting very dark and *Dresden* only just distinguishable. Flames 30 ft high are coming out of our funnels. At nine we turn round and are now going back to the rendezvous hoping to catch the collier there (the *Gotha*). If we can get her we can prevent the *Dresden* from obtaining coal and we may yet catch her. If only we had had the *Glasgow* or *Bristol* with us we could have settled the *Dresden* today. It's a melancholy thought. Wonder if the collier (who has wireless) has been scared away or no.

Tuesday March 9th. Return to rendezvous and wait there all day in hopes of meeting the colliers. Nothing happened, however.

Wednesday March 10th. Sailed afternoon for Coronel.

Thursday March 11th. Anchored at dawn off Santa Maria Island. The picket boat went into Coronel 12 miles away to order coal for us tomorrow. In the afternoon went away with Wharton blowing up fish. We went in the small whaler. The first charge of 2½ lb blew up some thousands of herring hake so that the sea was white with them for hundreds of yards round. So overwhelmed were we that we signalled for the steam picket boat to come out and help. We filled the boat with fish and we were all covered in slime from them. Brought back several thousand fish, enough for every man to have several. Wharton said he had never seen so many blown up before.

Friday March 12th. Coronel at dawn and coaling all day and night from lighters, very slow work. In the afternoon some of us accepted the invitation of a Mr Garner, the mining engineer of the coal company, 'the Minas Schwabe', to play tennis. The Consul took us ashore and we got into a special train and were taken north along the coast for several miles to the company settlement. The Garners' house was a pretty bungalow overlooking the sea on the side of a hill. Their garden very pretty with roses and dahlias, and real grass. The Pilot wanted to roll on it but was restrained. Mrs Garner met us and introduced her two daughters. A pretty dark girl of 20 and a very thick-legged girl of 12 who was great fun. Mabel, as we found her name to be, kept us all on the go with cheeky questions and allowing herself to be chased all over the gardens. The mother and her elder sister appeared a little jealous of her popularity. We adjourned soon to the court higher up the hill – a paved, tiled court cut out of the hill side, amidst lovely gardens and with a backing of giant gum trees, and with a view over the blue sea. Tennis was good again after so much ship life and tea full of fun. We sat and picked walnuts off a tree above our heads after, or explored the gardens. The flowers very beautiful, especially the datura tree, a mass of big lily blossoms the size of arums.

We got back by special train to Coronel to see the *Kent* anchored against a gorgeous crimson sunset and studded with lights. A most enjoyable day. The colliers great thieves here. Found yards of our ropes, etc., stowed away in the lighters ready to be taken away.

Saturday March 13th. Sailed 7 a.m. and proceeded west. Destination Juan Fernandez.

SINKING THE DRESDEN

Sunday/Monday March 14/15th. Full speed in the night ordered and so we arrived within sight of Juan Fernandez (MasAfuera) at daylight. Wireless was picked up from a German ship saying, 'I am at MasAfuera. Meet me here.' Whether it was *Dresden* calling for her collier or *vice versa*? I didn't know this, however, and awoke feeling an electrical something in the air, and scenting battle. So didn't put on No. 1. As we approached the island I saw it to be composed of high volcanic walls, the remains of an old crater evidently, and thickly wooded in places. The walls very thin for their height of about 3,000 ft. Soon we picked up the smoke of the *Glasgow* and later the *Orama*, 20 miles away straight ahead of us. The island lay ahead of us on our port bow. All three of us converged onto the island. As we rounded several points and nothing appeared the news went round that routine was to be as usual and so I went below to change my clothes. Half way through the act Action was sounded and in a second the ship was in a turmoil of sound. Never had I known the men respond so quickly, tumbling down the stairs in their eagerness. Then I heard the news shouted, 'the *Dresden* is lying in the Bay at anchor.' Hastily getting my water bottle I rushed on deck and there sure enough, lying in Cumberland Bay, half hidden against the cliffs behind her was a three-funnelled cruiser. The excitement for us all lay in wondering what was going to happen, would she open fire at us? Would we let her intern or would we open fire? The village lay directly behind her from where we were rushing in at her. I had to go below to my station and see if everything all O.K. I came up to inspect my ambulance parties, and while at this saw the *Dresden* again. She had run up the German flag at her fore and was getting up steam. I dived below again and shortly afterwards heard the order come through, 'Open fire'. The first salvo brought back the old smell of the Falklands Battle, even down to us below, and filled the passages with smoke. Salvo after salvo roared out above us but in four minutes all was over.

The *Dresden* had hoisted the white flag and the crew were leaving the ship in boats and going ashore. When I was able to get on deck again we were within a thousand yards of her. She was on fire after and amidships. Her after guns were dismantled. There was a huge hole in her starboard waterline aft, and her casemates were blown to pieces in two places. She was still at anchor and between her and the shore were a stream of boats filled with half-dressed men. By and by a steam boat flying a huge white flag came towards us. This carried the Captain of the *Dresden* and we directed him to the *Glasgow* as the senior ship. The *Glasgow* had by this time got into the bay followed by the *Orama*, and we soon all anchored about 1,000 yds from the *Dresden*. I am told that the German Captain demanded indignantly the reason why we fired at him at anchor in a neutral port. John Luce is said to have replied, 'I am sorry for you, but I had my orders and had no choice.' On the *Kent* we mostly felt rather uneasy at our deed, and wanted to know if she had fired first at us, and whether we had had orders to fire from the *Glasgow*. But anyhow our Captain isn't superior officer so we don't mind much. We hear that just as we opened fire she ran up a signal, put up in wrong order, however, 'We want to negotiate.'

Soon an order came. All doctors wanted ashore to attend to wounded. Just as Burn and I were ready to leave the ship there was a big explosion on the *Dresden* and smoke came from her port-side forward. Just previous to this a man had been seen to rush up on deck from below and, waving a boat away that was coming alongside for him, dive into the water and swim off to the boat. Evidently they had blown up her magazine. Then we got into the boat and were rowed ashore, passing close to the *Dresden* on the way and rather afraid of her exploding and damaging us. The water was strewn with hammocks, tubs, etc., and we passed close to a ?torpedo of theirs bobbing about. Arrived ashore; a native conducted us to a garden where a German doctor met us and asked me indignantly why we had fired on them. I shrugged my shoulders and passed in to the wounded. There were about 10 of them lying about, the ghastly results of modern shell fire, and all badly wounded. But first aid had been given to all these and we were sent on further to the verandah of a house where we met Fleet Surgeons Gilmour and Wizard and three other wounded. Then we set to work operating on the spot. Later, orders came to remove the wounded to the *Orama* so we simply made the other two comfortable and waited for stretchers.

It was a wonderful scene. We were on the verandah of a bungalow type of house. The owners of the house were standing round helping, and little children played between our legs or looked on wonderingly. They willingly lent sheets, pillows and got hot water and opened bottles of wine. They looked rough Chilean fisher folk. Behind us, the hill rose steeply to a sort of square where the Germans had by this time collected and were answering their names. Above this rose a precipice, thickly wooded, in the shape of a vast amphitheatre culminating in a *very* sharp peak about 3,000 ft high. The gardens around were filled with fruit trees and palms. But the scene in the bay was what fascinated us. The *Dresden* close in shore and sitting around her were our three ships watching her death struggles. She was visibly sinking now. The smoke still came out in curls from her amidships, and she was nearly awash when suddenly her nose plunged downwards. She gave a big heave over to port and we could see the water pouring down into her funnels, then her stern went under and the water boiled with the rush of the escaping air, then slowly her masts disappeared. While this was happening the Germans above us were cheering wildly and started to sing their National Anthem.

After this, I found two more wounded at other houses and saw to their embarking in our boats, which were then towed out (strange sight) to the *Orama* by the *German* steam boat. The *Dresden*'s skipper was on the beach looking on. A more villainous-looking face I don't hope to see. A great pendulous nose, coloured by many a carouse was not the least striking feature. He was very rude to one of our surgeons and turned his back on him.

A little man in khaki sporting rig came up to me on the beach. He was a Scots trader and arriving at Juan Fernandez and finding the *Dresden* there he had sent off news which was then on its way to Valparaiso to us. At 2 p.m. we returned to the *Kent* and had lunch and then Burn went back to the beach to try and find the Englishman. The P.M.O. and I went across to the *Orama* where we found Gilmour and the two *Orama*'s surgeons busy on a German lieutenant's leg, which I helped to amputate above the knee. The P.M.O. left after tea and arranged to send some of my things to the *Orama* and for me to go to Valparaiso with the wounded on the *Orama*. We worked on, with an interval for dinner, until midnight at compound fractures, etc., and then next morning started again and didn't finish until the late afternoon.

There were 12 badly wounded Germans and four not so serious. One lieutenant, one midshipman, an engineer and wireless man, and seamen. Without exception they were most brave and cheerful under their suffering. The lieutenant was assiduous in translating the requests of his men and generally looking after them, although he was in severe pain and must have felt the loss of his right leg and the consequent end of his career in the Navy. We made a point of being nice to them and they seemed very surprised and grateful for their treatment and on leaving the lieutenant insisted on leaving £1 (English gold), all he possessed, 'for the Red Cross'. The midshipman, who had a splinter in his leg, was not in the sick bay but occupied a cabin and he nearly cried when I took him some cigarettes.

Tuesday March 16th. At Valparaiso the doctors from the German Hospital came aboard and the Chilean Navy sent stretchers and bearers and the sick were transferred to launches alongside. It was a big business. Dr Münnich promised to let me know *via* the Consul how the wounded progressed.

In the afternoon I got ashore for two hours, with Captain Healey of the Orient liner *Orotava*. Valparaiso must have much of interest but there was no time for me to see it. Bought a Kodak tank machine and an old Peruvian copper jug. Would dearly like a month or two there, to visit Santiago, and Andes. By the evening the Germans in Valparaiso had got hold of their story from the wounded and promptly published a late edition of their paper giving it to the public very fairly, accurately too. About tea a Chilean lieutenant captain came aboard on behalf of the German

Consul General and asked for the bodies of three dead Germans whom he said we had still. We filled him up with cocktails, elicited the fact that the Chileans themselves were rather relieved than otherwise, and of course denied any corpse-keeping tendencies.

Hoped to have news of Norah here but no mails for us and papers up till Feb 13th had no notice of the birth.

AFTERMATH

Wednesday March 17th. Returning to Juan Fernandez.

Thursday March 18th. To meet the *Kent* at MasAfuera tomorrow. The life on the *Orama* was a very pleasant holiday and change after the *Kent*. To begin with the large decks gave plenty of exercise. The food was scrumptious and all the officers were most kind in making me at home.

Welham, the Senior Temporary Surgeon was an ex-P. & O. man and had spent 2 years with an American millionaire all over Europe and America. Scowcroft, the other, is a surgeon on one of the Cunard Boston boats. He served in the South Africa war and after that explored Malaya and the Far East. His tales of Cunard life very interesting. Must be a bit of a trial to the executive officers though, in the Cunard, from all accounts. He admitted to me that he hated all of them for their narrow outlook mostly. The Commander R.N.R. is Captain Healey who from commanding a similar ship in the Orient line descends in the *Orama* to the position of a helpless looker on with nothing to do, Captain Seagrave R.N. treating him, as all R.N.R. officers without the slightest tact or respect for their experience. Every officer in the ship complained to me of Seagrave's stupidity, obstinacy and rudeness to them. Carver, Lieutenant R.N.R. is an old Bristolian. There were several Canadians amongst the officers including Carver, and Heal a professional singer and entertainer. Assenheimer, the wit of the ship, had left his ranch and said he had forgotten to lock the door of his house.

I thoroughly enjoyed the change of new faces and fresh folk to talk to. Their stories of their Captain, the Swiss Ship's crew, the burning and abandoned German ship, etc., almost unbelievable.

Friday March 19th. Sighted MasAfuera early and anchored off the north-west and at midday under a great cliff 3,000 ft high. A most draughty spot it was too. All the winds of the Pacific seemed to eddy round the peaks above us. MasAfuera itself most interesting to me. Continual growls from every other officer on *Orama* and later the *Kent* as to the absolute lack of interest the place possessed. No accounting for tastes. It's a volcanic island – highest point 6,000 odd ft. Several peaks in a row, and the ground slants away to the north in series of plateaux and deep, water cut gullies ending in broader valleys near the sea. An old penal station on the shore opposite the largest valley. High up on the plateaux, 3,000 ft up, were little settlements amongst trees, approached by zigzag paths carried across the faces of cliffs and winding in and about the ridges to escape having to cross the gully-like valleys. The whole island covered with dried-up grass, and wooded on the steeper slopes. We could see no people, and I believe the island is uninhabited now, except by thousands of goats. We continually saw them standing on the edge of the great cliffs, large fellows with patriarchal beards and big horns. Every cloud for miles round seemed attached to the peaks inland and we constantly got little showers as the south wind blew them north. The whole time we were there, we never saw the highest summits though the 3,000 ft cliff was often quite clear and the sun quite strong.

As there was no sign of the *Kent* yet, I borrowed Captain Healey's fishing line and made him a stretcher and fitted up the line properly and commenced to fish. Healey himself had fished for six months without ever catching anything. Imagine his delight when I hauled in almost immediately a large bream of 5 lb. A little later I got a cavalli, a most sporting fish on the lines of an albacore, and with a yellow tail, which fought like a salmon. He was about 10 lb. A little later another cavalli broke my line half way up the ship's side. Result – immediate rush to make fishing lines all over the ship. The *Kent* came along at 4 p.m. making enough smoke with her Coronel coal to mask a fleet. I got aboard her in time for dinner and had a busy dinner answering questions as to latest news, etc.

Kent had seen nothing fresh at the rendezvous. Very sorry to leave the *Orama* for some things, but glad to get back to my belongings again as my stock of clothes was scanty.

Saturday March 20th. Fished all morning and got some bream but not much. In afternoon tried to get ashore after blowing up a lot of red (brilliant red) mullet. But close inshore the swell was too great to risk the boat so we contented ourselves with watching the thousands of small fish and a lobster. We dropped a lobster pot we had made but the small fish got in through the too-large mesh and devoured all the bait.

In the evening we commenced to catch small sharks about 3 ft long. In one of them I found 7 small sharks with their yolk sacs still suspended from their umbilicus. They were put into a bucket and swam about looking very funny, each with what looked like the yolk of an egg depending from its stomach. About 9 inches long each. We used them as bait for still more ground sharks.

A lantern lecture this evening by the Captain on Russo–Jap war.

Sunday March 21st. Coaling all day. This afternoon went away in the cutter with a volunteer crew to fish close inshore. We intended to fish for the tiny fish we had seen yesterday. We soon started, with all sorts of odd ends of line and various sized hooks. At first Redhead with a tiny gut hook got all the luck with small 'perch' and 'roach'. The big hookers were, at first, jealous but suddenly a Scots fisherman from the Highlands pulled in a 10 lb black fish and after that the big hookers carried the day. Every few seconds someone hauled in a fish. Part of the fun was that we could see the fish biting. The varieties were numerous. Then Howard caught an eel. A big brown snake speckled with white. It wriggled and tied knots in the line while Howard scrambled away from it as far as he could get. After that so many snakes came along that we moved our pitch. Dinner time came and found us very loath to return. Sport was too good. We got over 160 fish in two hours. Big 15 lb rock cod, black fish, 'bream', small yellow tails, 'perch', 'roach', red mullet, 'gurnard' (red), 'snakes'. I got a beautiful cavalli of 12 lb. It was an amusing afternoon. Nor did the Soldier forget to bring with him the sloe gin.

Monday March 22nd. Left in afternoon for rendezvous. *Orama* gone north to Mollendo and Lima. We hope to pick up *Orita* with mails off Valparaiso, and then go north ourselves to Callao.

Saturday March 27th. Arrived off Valparaíso after interminable days at sea. The whole ship suffering from reaction and having no definite objective. The weather getting wintry. Occasional strong south winds, rather cold. Not a ship seen. A most lonely part of the ocean directly you leave the coastal routes. Showed our noses just outside the three mile limit to scare the German steamers inside and then we patrol up and down the coast trying to get into wireless touch with the *Orita* and failing. We chase several ships, mostly Chilean coasters and a Japanese and generally feel bored to tears.

Tuesday March 30th. Boarded the *Orita* at last and of course she had no mails. But she gave us fresh food. However, we hear that the *Orama* leaves Valparaiso this afternoon for the north and she has mails for us. Therefore go north and wait in her track outside Valp. Board her at 8 p.m. by moonlight and at last our mails. I get a *Times* of Feb 17th first and see a notice in it of the birth of a son to us[10].

Later a letter from Grace Lane [author's mother-in-law] of the 17th giving the details. Two weeks mails, however, are missing. Probably in the *Macedonia*.

Everyone feeling better for their mails. Strange sounds of revelry from a certain cabin at midnight. My son to be called David Falkland then.

Wednesday/Thursday March 31st/April 1st. Going north 10 knots. Coaled yesterday at sea. Dented the collier some in doing so too. Off Valparaiso 4 days ago saw the strange sight of hundreds of lobsters on the surface swimming along by coming up every few seconds and shewing their feelers and diving again. Couldn't make

---

10 'DIXON. On the 15th inst. at 77, Pembroke Road, Clifton, the wife of Surgeon T.B. DIXON, R.N.V.R., H.M.S. Kent – a son.' The *Times* 17/2/15.

out for some time what they were, suggested cuttlefish, or sea weed with fish underneath.

Sunday April 4th. P.M.O. decided this a.m. couldn't leave our case of appendicitis a day longer. Operation by Burn in the afternoon. Large abscess. Boy rather bad this evening. Hope to land him in hospital at Callao.

Monday April 5th. *Orama* ordered us by wireless to meet her at San Nicholas. So we go south again and meet her there 6 p.m.

Tuesday April 6th. The bird life of this place is wonderful. Long lines of shag. 50,000 at one time we estimated. Pelicans by the thousand and many kinds of divers, gulls, seals and altogether there could not have been much less than a quarter of a million birds in sight. Fish must be very plentiful and yet I couldn't get a bite, expect I am too far out in the bay. The diving birds, pelicans, and others very fascinating to watch. They drop like streaks of white from about 30 ft and when a flock of them are doing it is a remarkable sight. They fold their wings completely and drop like stones. The pelicans make a splash like a 12 pounder shell.

In the afternoon a party went away with the seine [net] and brought back some mullet (grey). Would have got more if they hadn't chosen a place with a rocky bottom, and got it caught. Boy still seriously ill. (Coaled. Boy better, temperature normal[11].)

Wednesday April 7th. Proceeded at 8 a.m. to Callao.

Thursday April 8th. Arrived Callao 8 a.m. Went ashore with Wharton and Harvey. Bought fish hooks, ammonia, etc., [in] Callao, and took train to Lima. Fields all irrigated. Lima a fine city. Met Harry Woodhouse who took us to lunch at Mr and Mrs Hammond's, after putting up fizz at the club. The Hammonds most kind and put up a fine luncheon at a few minutes notice. Tried custard apples and passion fruit for the first time. The coffee wonderful. Table decorated with brilliant pink creeper

---

11   The boy recovered.

'Beaissima'. Japanese servants. The house, the old palace of a Spanish marquis. After lunch saw another old palace and then to the Cathedral to see the mummified remains of Pizzaro in his glass coffin. Bought an old silver mug for David Falkland. Got back in time to see the visitors on board before they left, Mrs Ashton, MacIver both there. Mrs Wingfield away. The snotties had a great time in the gun room. Crammed with fair young things.

We landed the appendix boy, Taylor, at the Italian Hospital where he was made very comfortable.

Friday April 9th. All day going south to San Nicholas again.

Saturday April 10th. Arrived daybreak. *Orama* finished coaling. In the afternoon party went ashore again with seine and choosing a sandy portion of the beach got a great haul of fish: skate, halibut, plaice, grey mullet, dog fish — enough for the whole ship's company. Extraordinary to think that all these fish are to be found within 30 yards of the beach. Large 5 lb fish too. In the evening went across with some of our officers and 200 odd men to the *Orama* to an entertainment they were giving. Held in their 1st class saloon. It was first class all the way through. The one act farce quite good too. Hadn't laughed so much for months. Heal who trained the performers is a professional singer and entertainer. After the show we adjourned to Smoking Room and drinks flowed along. We started dancing to a fine bagpipes and finished up about midnight with a football scrum after lancers. It was a great night and improved the relations between the two ships.

Sunday April 11th. Proceeding north to Callao to meet *Orita* who has food for us.

Monday April 12th. Meet *Orita* at 6 p.m. outside Callao and get potatoes, meat, etc. Caught an albacore this morning on the boom gear, about 8 lb.

Tuesday April 13th. Proceeding north to Paita and after that to Galapagos.

Tuesday April 27th. Fortnight later. We went leisurely north and after some days anchored in Sechura Bay. A vast open bay, the horns of which could just be seen each from the other. We *anchored* 7 miles out. The bay filled with the quaintest fishing rafts made of driftwood, some large and carrying huge sails and a family, others quite small of two to four logs made to carry one or two people only. A big paddle was used as a drop keel by jamming down between the logs amidships. They looked such fascinatingly primitive craft that the Commander tried to buy one. But as there was no way of landing the owners, we had to arrange to get them to bring another raft next day for £1 sail and all. They turned up punctually next morning as agreed. The Indian owners came aboard and having begged some thread proceeded to sit down on the quarter-deck and twist it into stouter thread holding the thread meanwhile in a most funny manner with their toes. Then they sewed and rigged up a sail. They were short immensely strong figures, very Japanese to look at and handsome in a Japanese way, quite brown with black hair coarse almost as quills. When, elated with our purchase, we tried to move the raft by means of the ungainly paddle they simply shrieked with laughter. The 'boat' would be useful for the Galapagos if we were to go there for landing in surf, or fishing inshore.

After coaling we proceeded to Paita and anchored in that desolate dried-up bay early one morning. We were curtly told, however, by the Captain of the Port we mustn't land or buy anything. No boats were allowed to come near the ship either. He alleged orders from Lima. Real explanation being he got into trouble over the visit of the Japanese warship *Osama* earlier in the war and was taking no risks now. Payta looked a dried up collection of adobe houses, but is the port of an oil field and so is important. Caught dozens of small 'grunt' which fried nicely next a.m. No fresh food now left in ship, since Payta failed us. No news of supply ship. The men are living on *dry bread* and tea for breakfast, tea and supper, as there is nothing in the canteen. *Orama* won't ask for supply ship. Reasons we can guess at but mustn't say. Our only hope is that we may be allowed to buy provisions at Lima.

We returned to Sechura Bay and met the *Orama* and a new collier the *Eggesford*, Captain Johnson of whom looks a good fellow. His patent traverse table[12] should do well. Went away while we were here one afternoon in the Captain's galley, a fine graceful boat with two sails. Took some snotties and fished off a bank and caught some fine fish. Lent the snotties some lines and hooks. They never troubled to return them to me properly cleaned or put up, with the exception of 3 of them, they are a lousy lot. Lying out at full length in the galley sailing along delightfully pleasant. Had a race another afternoon with the Captain. I was in the German boat from the *Dresden* rechristened the *Invicta* and owing to superior tacking powers easily beat the skipper. The *Invicta*, a 20 footer, is a fine little craft.

We made our way south at last to Lima, practising night attack one evening with searchlights, for the first time this commission, on the collier.

Monday April 26th [Written after last entry.] Arrived Lima. Allowed to take provisions. The answering salute from the Peruvian shore batteries stopped at 7 guns. Three different explanations given by the three different officials. Real reason alleged to be they have no ammunition. Cricket match arranged with the locals for the afternoon. After lunch I went up to Lima to see Dr Merandez about a stopping for a front tooth. He was a dear old chap and put in any amount of time and trouble, and made a very good job indeed and would only take half fees. Got back in time to help entertain guests on board to tea, and found the mail had arrived. Had given up hopes of it too. Letters up to March 14th. Norah apparently had a bad time. Everyone seems to have been most kind to her.

The Lima folk sent 100 gallons of beer on board for the crew and gave them an awfully good entertainment including a cinema in the evening. Both much appreciated. I got Johnson to stay to dinner along with the entertainment party. We had an uproarious time. Monsieur Stockman, the Belgian Vice Consul, nearly wept when we drank King Albert's health and made a great speech in French. After the entertainment some of the cricketers who had dined ashore came home to roost. The scenes on the quarter-deck were immense. Old Stockman with his patriarchal beard trying to

12 Navigational aid.

waltz with our 'very sober' Captain of Marines, and cannoning off each other's abdomens. Enter an exhilarated doctor from his shore dinner, strokes the old Belgian beard and gets kissed on both cheeks affectionately. Visions of a certain stout officer trying to settle his bill with the contractor, two ladies overloaded themselves trying to rescue their husbands from the cocktail party below. The cinema proprietor, who didn't know one word of English, got so excited that he had to be allowed to speechify for fear he would burst if hold in! He declared he wouldn't charge for his show he had been treated so well. Alas we lost the cricket match by an innings. The shore dinner party had a great time. They dined at the chief restaurant in Lima with some friends and getting worked up started to make speeches. 'The whole of Lima' meanwhile looked on from the other tables and the street. Then the *Kent* started an entertainment, club swinging with champagne bottles. The Pilot then showed how he could jump the whole length of the table with everyone sitting thereat, and other acrobatics. Meanwhile, the band had got enthused . . . Hungarian girl band I'm told . . . and played *Tipperary* and music for Burn to do his funny dances. The spectators were most enthusiastic. Finally the Pilot, seizing a huge bouquet from the table, climbed up the side of the restaurant up to the balcony where the band lived and on bended knee presented it to the leading lady of the band. Great enthusiasm. Exchange of hats in the train with Peruvian officer. Jones, one hit stunt on the pier, etc., etc. It will be long before Lima forgets the *Kent*. We are simply loved here. Johnson promised to get me some vicuña furs for my wife.

Wednesday/Thursday April 28th/29th. Proceeded north to Sechura Bay again where we meet the *Orama*. Got introduction from Assenheimer of *Orama* to people at Esquimalt. Coaled.

Friday April 30th. At Sechura fishing and sailing.

Saturday May 1st. Sailed north for Cocos Islands. Each day became hotter and when we got to the line we entered the doldrums, no wind to speak of and heavy rain clouds which burst first one night about 2 a.m. The confusion on deck at first was comic. All the men slinging in hammocks on deck swearing at having got wet and having to go below. The rain came down in sheets. Commander B. and Commander W., Padre and myself danced about on the quarter-deck in the rain with 'nodings on' enjoying a bath, while the lightning played around. A weird sight. The sea water was now no longer cold from the Peruvian Current and it got steadily hotter till we got to the Cocos.

The *Orama* had visited the Galapagos while we went to Lima. They reported it intensely hot, no breeze on the north side. The Islands covered with very dense scrub, populated with wild donkeys, snakes, lizards, sea lions and sharks. Captain Seagrave shot a sea lion which he kept frozen in the cold storage! A number of the crew got sunstroke. They didn't seem to have enjoyed their visit much. The *Kent* would have known how to much better and it's a pity we did not go there. They said the clouds of birds were so tame as to be a nuisance, coming and settling on one's walking stick, etc.

Thursday May 6th. Sighted the Cocos Islands early, and, soon after, the masts of the *Newcastle* waiting there for us. Anchored at 1 p.m. in Cumberland Bay. The weather very close and threatening black clouds to west. Commenced to coal at once from our collier and then storm broke. We coaled in the wet as it continued to rain all day. The *Newcastle* looked very neat if small. She had had a very good time up north at Esquimalt and said they were all waiting to welcome the *Kent* up there. The Island of Cocos is thick with trees and bush including lots of coconuts. It's very hilly, rising up to 2,700 ft, almost every square inch covered with almost impenetrable green. The air coming off the Island smelt heavy with tropic scents, sandal wood, etc., and over each cliff a waterfall tumbled. Uninhabited, it had retained traces of the party that came here a year or two back to hunt for treasure buried by the old buccaneers who made it their headquarters. There was a zig-zag visible up through one of the green cliffs rising from the beach, evidently cut by man, though nearly overgrown. We were unable to land, much to my disappointment as we pushed on up north the same evening. The birds very tame. A sort of booby bird came settling by dozens everywhere and we caught many of them. No fish caught, though tried for in 30 fathoms. Wild pig abound on shore.

Friday May 7th. Increasingly hot. Sweltering on the mess decks at night. Turtles seen, often asleep on the water. One with a bird perched on his back. Whales spout around us.

Thursday May 13th. Arrived at Socorro Island at dawn. We had heard by cable at Paita (*via* originally we were told the Japanese Ambassador at Stockholm!) that there was a suspicious vessel using Socorro as a base for something or other. Sure enough the vessel was there anchored – a small oil tanker of about 1,000 tons. The island loomed up behind her brown and barren looking, to a rocky summit inland about 3,000 ft. It was covered with what looked like mown grass, green in the hollows and higher up inland. Evidently of volcanic origin. We boarded the 'pirate', his story was that he was taking oil to Java and was waiting here for another vessel. His papers were in order. He had an extreme list to starboard. He told us of countless wild sheep ashore and millions of fish, and was very affable. He was evidently a German or Dutchman originally, but claimed to be American, his boat The ? of Los Angeles. The boarding party came back and told their tale. Meanwhile exploring parties were being got up. The Captain kindly lent me his galley to go away fishing. Others went ashore to reconnoitre the camp of the 'pirates'. In the galley we had *the* sport of the commission. We rowed inshore close to the rocks under a high lava cliff, and immediately my line was down caught a small multicoloured fish. This was the prelude to dozens more of all shapes and colours. The colours unbelievable unless seen. Bright primary colours. One fish, for instance, bright red all over with a complete edging of a band of Reckitts blue, $\frac{1}{6}$ inch wide. Another with a bump on the top of his head and quaint projecting teeth two below and two above.

I had lent the boat's crew lines and soon we began to lose hooks, big fish evidently about. Then I hauled in a 15 lb rock cod. Next, on pulling up a smaller fish weighing about 2 lb a big 20 lb rock cod followed him up and swallowed him whole. I got the two. This gave us a hint and after this we used the largest cod hooks and whole fish for bait and promptly caught whoppers 15–20 lb rock cod and several small sharks. A big shark then took my hook and bait. I lost him just as he was coming inboard and we returned to the ship to lunch and to get stronger lines and more hooks. The shore party reported nothing found except signs of recent living.

After dinner we went back to our fishing spot and all the afternoon hauled up big cod fish until our arms ached. We caught also a black charynx, and a conger. These congers were a nuisance and by taking the bait and retreating to their holes we lost a lot of line and hooks. We returned to tea laden with so much fish that the whole ship's company were able to have some. After tea we returned to pick up our anchor which had jammed and got a few more. It is remarkable how close to the shore the fish are in these Pacific Islands. We fished twenty yards only from the rocks in 6 fathoms. From the ship only ½ mile out practically nothing was caught.

In the afternoon shooting parties and a seining party left the ship. They beat the hill sides and found sheep. We heard salvos and rapid independent [fire] going on and later they brought back 10 sheep and one living lamb which bleated pathetically. The party reported the going as atrocious; cinders, lava holes, brushwood and cacti. The guns and their beaters were covered with bruises from falls and studded with cactus prickles. The seine could not be used owing to rocks and so the galley's haul was all the more admired and appreciated. The lamb is a ram and feeds on condensed milk from a bottle and teat.

General opinion is that Socorro is a sporting place and we should like to stop a week. Next day we steamed out of the bay and round the corner out of the 3 mile limit and then returned suddenly to anchorage. The 'pirates' were surprised presumably, but we had no means of proving this. But we sent off another boarding party who explored the hold this time but returned with the same story of nothing wrong. General opinion is that the ship is engaged in running guns for the Mexicans. But she might be a potential oil base for a submarine. Anyway the Mexican Navy now know of her as we wirelessed to them.

We left that afternoon again for San Bartolomé.

(Gave my lantern lecture on Swiss Alpine climbing. Think it went well.)

Friday/Sautrday May 14th/15th. Making for the scene of the *Osama*'s (Japan) accident. She ran onto a rock, right in the entrance to the harbour of San Bartolomé. U.S. Survey showed no rock. It's like those careless devils. The *Osama* went ashore in January. Salvage ship from Japan has just floated her after 100 days.

Monday May 17th. Arrived 7 a.m. H.M.S. *Rainbow* from Esquimalt there also. *Osama, Shitushi* (repair ship) and collier (English).

The bay is well sheltered very shallow and the land all round it dry as a bone with a few of the giant cacti. Mountains everywhere in the distance. Typical Mexican desert. A small fishing village inhabited by Japanese on shore. Products: fish, *turtles*. The Jap fishers have a fine motor boat and a barque.

Usual formal visits from and to the other ships. The Japanese very interesting. Their get up spotless. Their picket boat exact copy of our type, sparkling with polish and the *little* 'boys' in sailor suits stood up smartly at the bow and handled our paintwork carefully with the butt of their boathooks. So different to our slapdash untidy R.N.R. fishermen!

We coaled 500 tons and in the afternoon visited the *Osama* and were shewn round the damaged cruiser. It's marvellous how they have repaired the whole ship's bottom, taken out boilers and engines and built in extra bulkheads with only the loss of life of one diver. Every man aboard was as clean as a pin, in whites too, in spite of living in all the upset of a salvage job – in half their usual amount of room and twice the crew. In the evening four officers and some middies came to us. They were all eager to hear all about our fighting but couldn't speak much English although they understood it.

Attempts afterwards to make them drink in the ward room rather a failure. They sat and toyed with their crème de menthe but hardly touched it.

The *Rainbow* included old friends for several of our officers. They gave us much information on Esquimalt, and loaded us with the loan of tennis racquets, golf clubs, rods, etc. She is an old ship of ours taken over by the Canadian Navy and filled with a 'nondescript crowd of retired R.N.R. farmers from the backwoods'. She is to patrol the Mexican coast *pro tem*. Her officers gave us a turtle, a fine large one. We gave the Japanese our pig Dennis now grown hugely fat and of dirty habits – to be eaten as a relish to their rice. As an old ship mate we couldn't eat him ourselves.

No fish caught. The Japanese have blown up too many in the harbour. They exploded an old torpedo war-head once and got, amongst others, a rock cod of 120 lb.

Tuesday May 18th. North 10½ knots to Vancouver, and into quite cold, rough weather. North wind and huge swell, which being head-on makes the *Kent* pitch badly, but not as badly as she can roll. Still, screws come out of the water and race and shake my cabin badly. To stand at the stern and watch the waves, one second level with the deck and the next 40 feet below you, is a grand sight.

The lamb flourishes and now eats cheese, sardines and potato peelings. He knows the butcher and follows him everywhere.

The turtle interesting. His back bleeding where it was scratched. Killed by cutting off the head and hanging up by the hind flappers to bleed. Turtle soup very good. Turtle steak not unlike veal, very tender, but needs a little bacon with it really.

Wednesday May 19th. Very rough still.

Thursday May 20th. Fine weather. Sea calmer.

Friday/Saturday May 21st/22nd. Beautiful calm seas and warm sunshine, a bite in the air to keep us alive. Just like an English spring. Sighted (on Sat 22nd) Cape Mendocino. A big sooty albatross very common the last 3 days. Just like the southern hemisphere variety but sooty instead of white. The wireless news on this coast most absurd stuff. Starts each day with – Balls – and goes on to justify the term. Balls means baseball games really.

The last 5 days we have sailed continually through myriads of small nautili[13]. First day they were about 3 or 4 to the square yard, the size of a chestnut. On Friday, off 'Frisco, we entered great fields of them so thick that they lay on top of each other and made big

13   A mollusc.

patches of purply *green* scum on the water. No-one aboard had ever seen anything like their numbers before. Billions upon billions of them. In the evening sun it looked as if had rained pearls, each nautilus sail glistening.

Looked at from above the base was purple and the sail set diagonally across it was light green.

Spent 6 weeks at Esquimalt refitting. June 1915. After proceeding to the Gulf of Southern California we called in on one or two Mexican ports. Mazatlan one of them. Dankwerts (Gunnery Lieutenant) was landed at Lima with a hydatid abscess of lung, and until February 1916 when we arrived at Falklands again, we patrolled the South American Pacific coast. From Port Stanley we sailed to South Georgia to look for Shackleton. No news of him till a day or two after we had left. When he turned up at the whaling station we had just left. See Shackleton's *South*. Arrived Simons Town, Easter Sunday 1916.

Nine months patrolling and convoy duties between the Cape and Dakar, finished with *Kent* getting home to Plymouth January 1917.

When I did get home, David, who was two, took one look at me and then said to his mother, with obvious disappointment, 'Is *that* Daddy?'[14] [See Introduction.]

----

14 Recounted in a letter from T. B. Dixon to a friend. 7/1/57.

APPENDIX I

South Atlantic Naval Battle: Bristol Doctor's Graphic Account
(Western Daily Press, January 23, 1915)

SOUTH ATLANTIC NAVAL BATTLE

BRISTOL DOCTOR'S GRAPHIC ACCOUNT.

VIEWED FROM H.M.S. KENT.

Dr. Dixon, of the Bristol Dispensary, who was on H.M.S. Kent during the dramatic engagement off the Falkland Islands, has sent the following graphic account home:—

"This account is necessarily not at all complete—various confidential facts having to be kept back—but there is nothing untrue in it.

"The Kent joined up with the rest of the fleet at our base and waited the arrival of Admiral Sturdee in the battle cruiser Invincible, accompanied by the sister ship, the Inflexible. These two ships had come out secretly from England, and after only one day's delay to coal, proceeded towards the Falkland Islands with the Carnarvon, Cornwall, Kent, Bristol, Glasow, and the Macedonia, making a wide sweep for any German vessels.

"Arrived at the Falkland Islands early on Monday, December 7, we proceeded to coal at once, within a few minutes of anchoring. The Kent did not, but kept guard, ready to go out at once if necessary. This businesslike hurry was to prove very useful to us next day. Next morning, before breakfast, the look-out on the island signal station detected two cruisers steering hard from the direction of Cape Horn towards Port Stanley. At the same time we intercepted German wireless signals.

"The Kent put out at once towards the entrance of the harbour, and as we passed the flagship we saw the crew scurrying all over her, throwing off the hawsers from their collier and preparing for battle. The position for us on the Kent was a dramatic one. Over the low ridge of sand dunes to our south we could see the thick smoke of two vessels moving very rapidly towards the point, and suddenly there shot round into view a four-funnelled cruiser, which turned out to be the Gneisenau, followed by the three-funnelled Nürnberg. Just previous to this, however, the Canopus, right within the inner harbour, opened fire with her 12-inch guns, and although the first shots fell short, the effect on the cruisers was electrical, because the shots apparently came from nowhere—the old Canopus firing over the land between her and the enemy and being quite out of sight, and yet able to fire accurately owing to certain preparations made weeks beforehand. The enemy sheered off at once, but were able to get a view down the harbour before turning tail, and what they saw there gave them the surprise of their lives. We heard afterwards from an officer of the Nürnberg that they had heard we had abandoned the Falklands and fled to the West coast of Africa. When, therefore, they got hit by a shot from the Canopus and saw soon afterwards a fleet waiting for them, and thought also they detected Dreadnought cruisers amongst that fleet, they realised it was no place to loiter near, and turned tail and fled, signalling frantically to the Leipsic, Dresden and Scharnhorst, which were further out at sea, but plainly visible from the land.

"I was in a casemate when they came round into view, and could plainly see the Gneisenau's guns trained on to us. Every second we expected to see her open fire on us, but soon it became evident they were both running away, and we put out in chase. For some time we were at action stations, but as it became evident that battle wasn't imminent, we came up at 10 a.m. further to prepare ship for action.

"The scene was one to live in the memory. On deck were men flooding decks, breaking up wood which was going down to feed the hungry furnaces, and everyone had a broad smile and was most amazingly cheerful. The luck so much against us at Valparaiso was most certainly with us now. The weather was just perfect—a dead calm sea, brilliant light, the whole day before us for our job, and the tools handy. Behind us the mountains rose up higher as we got away from the land. The two battle cruisers came hurtling along, belching inky oil smoke, their white bow waves making a beautiful contrast to it. Behind them again were our other ships moving out of harbour. The weather was distinctly cold, but that again was good for fighting. To those who know the appalling weather conditions of these islands, the fact of our getting a fine day seemed almost a miracle in our favour. At eleven o'clock we went to early lunch, and enjoyed it, too. I was able to get a lot of photos of interest about this time, both on board and of the other ships. The battle cruisers passed us on our starboard, a grand sight—to us, if not the Germans. We heard afterwards that on board the Gneisenau they tried hard to persuade themselves they could not be Dreadnought cruisers. They thought they might be Japanese ships, and when they

had to admit them to be what they were, the ship's company went to prayers, realising that it meant defeat in all human probability—defeat and death. To us the enemy's ships appeared strung out in line abreast, steering S.E. Our two big ships were ahead of us. The Glasgow came on our port-bow, and behind us on our starboard quarter our sister ship came, the Cornwall. As the Inflexible and Invincible caught up with them, their quarry altered course to port, and strung out into line ahead. Our two followed suit, and converged on them, the two getting nearer and nearer.

"The excitement on the Kent was intense. Everyone not at work in the stokeholds, &c., gathered on the fo-cstle. I chose a seat on the top of the fore turret, and was able to draw rough plans of the movements of the fleets. Suddenly, at 12.55 a.m., we saw a great puff of dirty yellow smoke blow out from the Inflexible, and a great roar of cheering broke out from the men below me—the fight had started. It seemed ages before the shot dropped, in reality it was 35 seconds, and it fell short, evidently aimed at the last ship to the right of their line. The next shots were very close, and the enemy's ship aimed at suddenly veered off to starboard and fled away to the S.S.E.

"Our ships then turned their fire on to Nos. 2 and 3 in the line, the Scharnhorst and Gneisenau, still in extreme danger. At 1.30 the two Germans opened fire, a most dramatic movement, and their salvos were splendidly fired, all the guns together. A roar went up from our boys when it was seen that the Germans were short. Then the Gneisenau and Scharnhorst turned to port towards our line, while the other two light cruisers turned to starboard, and fled after their sister. The Kent, Cornwall, and Glasgow turned to starboard in chase, and immediately we went to our stations for action again, until we had passed the Gneisenau on our port, and were out of range, when we came up to get another view.

"On our port horizon we could see the Inflexible and Invincible hindering their two opponents, who were firing extremely well in return. The big splashes made by the falling shot were plainly visible all around each vessel. We watched them disappear on the horizon, going S.E.E.

"At 3 o'clock we could only see the smoke of one German, and reckoned one was sunk. Then we turned our attention to starboard. Here, on our bow, was the Glasgow, which had come across from our port side, and had overhauled one of the enemy lagging behind the other two. This turned out to be the Leipsic. She opened fire on the Leipsic, and fell short. Soon after both of them were fighting hard, and, not altogether to our surprise, the Leipsic's guns seemed to carry as far as the Glasgow's. Suddenly we all saw a flash of light on the Leipsic on her disengaged side, and we yelled ourselves hoarse—it was evidently a hit.

"It was intensely interesting watching a battle at such close quarters. At 4.30, having got within range ourselves, we opened fire on the Leipsic from the fore turret, taking her on her port quarter, the Glasgow on her starboard quarter, and we went to stations again. Our own battle had begun. The Cornwall came up soon after this, and so we passed on in chase of the Nürnberg, and soon began to overhaul her, too. At 5.15 we opened fire. She replied very accurately indeed; her firing that day was most accurate. Down below we could hear and feel the shells hitting us easily, in spite of the noise of our own guns. Hereabouts we became busy dressing some wounded, and while I was engaged on a man with a shell splinter through his chest, a shell came through the side of the Kent, and burst above the hatchway with a deafening din. We were all blown backwards, and there was a beastly smell of lyddite fumes. One man had his legs taken off by this, but no one else was injured. Later a shell burst in a casemate, and caused our chief

loss. The range now was quite close and the noise deafening, and we were being hit some; but the enemy was on fire, and ceased shooting soon after. After an interval she started firing again, and reluctantly we were forced to silence her altogether with what must have been a hazardous fire to her. Some time after six o'clock she ceased fire again, and hauled down her flag. We approached her, and when within 1,000 yards she turned on her side, funnels towards us, and sank in a few minutes. We steered down amongst the survivors, but could only manage to save seven alive. Our boats were too damaged to use except one we patched up hurriedly. Certainly some of our officers got into the water to endeavour to save life.

"The Kent had six killed and ten wounded. She had engaged two ships, one of them entirely on her own, which she sank. The Leipsic was sunk by the Cornwall and the Gloucester. The Dresden escaped owing to her speed. There was no vital damage done to the ship, although we have numerous holes in the funnels and deck-houses, where they do not matter. The Leipsic's captain came on deck at the end, and refused to haul down the flag, and sat smoking cigarettes till he went down with his ship. The Scharnhorst sank first of the other two, and not one survivor was picked up. The Gneisenau sank soon after, and the Inflexible picked up nearly a hundred of the crew. Our losses in the fleet were trifling. The Inflexible lost one man killed, the Invincible nobody. The Glasgow one killed and a few wounded, the Cornwall none. The enemy fought splendidly, but were quite outclassed."

APPENDIX II

Naval List for 1914, 1915 and 1916

Nov. 1914

271 KENT. *Cruiser.*
  9.800 *Tons. I.H.P.* 22.000 *N.D.*
  Guns – 14-6 *inch*, 8-12 *pr.*, 3-3 *pr.*
  Portsmouth

Captain	John D. Allen	— Sept 14
Commander	(I) Arthur E. F. Bedford	28 Aug 14
Lieut.-Com.	(T) Eric L. Wharton	6 Sept 14
	(N) James R. Harvey	8 Sept 14
Lieutenant	(G) Victor H. Danckwerts	25 Aug 14
Lieut.-Com. R.N.R.	Charles M. Redhead, RD.	16 Sept 14
Lieut. R.N.R.	Harold T. Dunn	16 Sept 14
	Frederic C. Howard	3 Oct 14
	William G. B. Jones	16 Sept 14
	Walter R. Tilling	3 Oct 14
	James Marshall	16 Sept 14
	John L. S. G. Lilley (*act*)	16 Sept 14
Eng. Com.	George E. Andrew	16 Sept 13
Eng. Lieut.-Com.	Alfred E. E. Rayner	2 Sept 14
Eng. Lieut. (ret)	Victor. O. Foreman	9 Sept 14
Capt. R.M.	Robert W. J. Laing	3 Oct 14
Chaplain	Rev. Norman B. Kent, BA (*act*)	3 Oct 14
Fleet Surg. (Ret.)	Edward B. Pickthorn	3 Oct 14
Paymaster	Sydney G. Andrews	6 Sept 14
Temp. Surg.	Ronald E. B. Burn	3 Oct 14
Surg. R.N.V.R.	Thomas B. Dixon	3 Oct 14
Asst. Paym. R.N.R.	William G. Stewart	22 Sept 14

Gunner	Thomas P. Collins	9 Mar 14
	Claude H. Griffiths (*act*)	— Sept 14
	(For Instructional Duties.)	
Boatswain	William T. Dunning	— Aug 14
	Walter H. Speed (*act*)	3 Oct 14
	(For Q.D. Duties.)	
Sig. Boatswain	Leonard C. Croucher (*act*)	— Sept 14
Carpenter	William H. Venning	23 Dec 11
Artif. Eng.	William Muirhead	27 Sept 14
Wt. Engineer R.N.R.	John Garrow	29 Aug 14
	John W. Scott (*a*)	— Sept 14
	Donald Campbell	13 Sept 14
Midshipman R.N.R.	Robert L. Burridge (*proby.*)	3 Oct 14
	John D. Ross (*proby.*)	3 Oct 14
	David T. M. Williams (*proby.*)	3 Oct 14
	George C. B. Liley (*proby.*)	3 Oct 14
	Cecil B. Hogan (*proby.*)	3 Oct 14
	Harold W. S. Wright (*proby.*)	3 Oct 14
	Frederick E. Valentine (*proby.*)	3 Oct 14
	George W. Barker (*proby.*)	3 Oct 14
	Edgar H. Cowan (*proby.*)	3 Oct 14
Clerk	Reginald H. Kitchin	22 Sept 14

Jan. 1915.

271 KENT. *Cruiser*
9,800 *Tons.* I.H.P. 22,000 N.D.
Guns – 14-6 *inch*, 8-12 *pr.*, 3-3 *pr.*
Portsmouth

Captain	John D. Allen	— Sept 14
Commander	(I) Arthur E. F. Bedford	28 Aug 14
Lieut.-Com.	(T) Eric L. Wharton	6 Sept 14
	(N) James R. Harvey	8 Sept 14
Lieutenant	(G) Victor H. Danckwerts	25 Aug 14
Lieut.-Com. R.N.R.	Charles M. Redhead, RD.	16 Sept 14
Lieut. R.N.R.	Harold T. Dunn	16 Sept 14
	Frederic C. Howard	3 Oct 14
	William G. B. Jones	16 Sept 14
	Walter R. Tilling	3 Oct 14
	James Marshall	16 Sept 14
	John L. S. G. Lilley (*act*)	16 Sept 14

Eng. Com.	George E. Andrew	16 Sept 13
Eng. Lieut. (ret)	Osborne W. Skinner	24 Nov 14
	Victor O. Foreman	9 Sept 14
Capt. R.M.	Robert W. J. Laing	3 Oct 14
Chaplain	Rev. Norman B. Kent, BA *(act)*	3 Oct 14
Fleet Surg. (Ret.)	Edward B. Pickthorn	3 Oct 14
Paymaster	Sydney G. Andrews	6 Sept 14
Temp. Surg.	Ronald E. B. Burn	3 Oct 14
Surg. R.N.V.R.	Thomas B. Dixon	3 Oct 14
Asst. Paym. R.N.R.	William G. Stewart	22 Sept 14
Gunner	Thomas P. Collins	9 Mar 14
	Claude H. Griffiths *(act)*	— Sept 14

(*For Instructional Duties.*)

Boatswain	William T. Dunning	— Aug 14
	Walter H. Speed *(act)*	3 Oct 14

(*For Q.D. Duties.*)

Sig. Boatswain	Leonard C. Croucher *(act)*	— Sept 14
Carpenter	William H. Venning	23 Dec 11
Artif. Eng.	William Muirhead	27 Sept 14
Wt. Engineer R.N.R.	John Garrow	29 Aug 14
	John W. Scott *(a)*	— Sept 14
	Donald Campbell	13 Sept 14
Midshipman R.N.R.	Robert L. Burridge *(proby.)*	3 Oct 14
	Ivor N. Ross *(proby.)*	3 Oct 14
	David T. M. Williams *(proby.)*	3 Oct 14
	George C. B. Liley *(proby.)*	3 Oct 14
	Cecil B. Hogan *(proby.)*	3 Oct 14
	Harold W. S. Wright *(proby.)*	3 Oct 14
	Frederick E. Valentine *(proby.)*	3 Oct 14
	George W. Barker *(proby.)*	3 Oct 14
	Edgar H. Cowan *(proby.)*	3 Oct 14
Clerk	Reginald H. Kitchin	22 Sept 14

Feb. 1916.

271 KENT. *Cruiser. (Po.)*
9,800 *Tons. I.H.P.* 22,000 *N.D.*
Guns – 14-6 *inch.* 8-12 *pr.*, 3-3 *pr.*

Captain	John D. Allen, CB	— Sept 14
Commander	(I) Arthur E. F. Bedford	28 Aug 14
Lieut.-Com.	(T) John H. Young	23 Mar 15

	(N) James R. Harvey	8 Sept 14
Lieutenant	(G) Robert C. Woollerton	30 Aug 15
Lieut.-Com. R.N.R.	Charles M. Redhead, RD.	16 Sept 14
Lieut. R.N.R.	Harold T. Dunn	16 Sept 14
	Frederic C. Howard	3 Oct 14
	William G. B. Jones	16 Sept 14
	Walter R. Tilling	3 Oct 14
	James Marshall	16 Sept 14
Eng. Com.	George E. Andrew, CB	16 Sept 13
Eng. Lieut.-Com. (ret)	Osborne W. Skinner	24 Nov 14
Capt. R.M.	Robert W. J. Laing	3 Oct 14
Chaplain	Rev. Norman B. Kent, BA (*act*)	3 Oct 14
Fleet Surg. (Ret.)	Edward B. Pickthorn	3 Oct 14
Paymaster	Sydney G. Andrews	6 Sept 14
Surg. R.N.V.R.	Thomas B. Dixon	3 Oct 14
Act. Sub-Lieut.	Robert L. Burridge (*act*)	3 Oct 14
R.N.R.	Frederick E. Valentine (*act*)	3 Oct 14
Asst. Paym. R.N.R.	Henry F. Gurney	22 Oct 15
Gunner	Thomas P. Collins	9 Mar 14
	Claude H. Griffiths	— Sept 14

(*For Instructional Duties.*)

| *Boatswain* | William T. Dunning | — Aug 14 |
| | Walter H. Speed | 3 Oct 14 |

(*For Q.D. Duties.*)

	Herbert Le Noury (*act*)	17 Sept 15
	Peter T. Newcomb (*act*)	17 Sept 15
	William J. S. Ashford (*act*)	17 Sept 15
Sig. Boatswain	Thomas E. Murtagh (*act*)	27 Apr 15
Carpenter	William H. Venning, DSC	23 Dec 11
Artif. Eng	William Muirhead	27 Sept 14
	Herbert J. Woods	— Nov 14
Wt. Engineer R.N.R.	John Garrow	29 Aug 14
	John W. Scott (*a*)	— Sept 14
	Donald Campbell	13 Sept 14
Midshipman R.N.R.	Ivor N. Ross (*proby.*)	3 Oct 14
	David T. M. Williams (*proby.*)	3 Oct 14
	Cecil B. Hogan (*proby.*)	3 Oct 14
	A. M. Marsden Jones	22 Oct 15
	Harold W. S. Wright (*proby.*)	3 Oct 14
	George W. Barker (*proby.*)	3 Oct 14
	Edgar H. Cowan (*proby.*)	3 Oct 14
Clerk	Reginald H. Kitchin	22 Sept 14

APPENDIX III

Illustrated list of British Ships involved in the
Battle of the Falklands.

Ships given in *italic* are those
mentioned in the text.

INVINCIBLE Class battle-cruisers

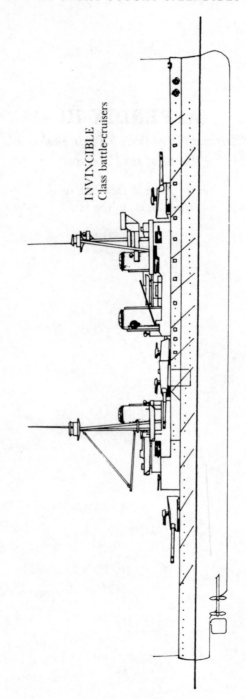

INVINCIBLE
Class battle-cruisers

INDOMITABLE, INFLEXIBLE, INVINCIBLE, all 1907

17,250 tons 567' (o/a) × 78½' × 25¾'. Guns 8 12", 16 4", 13". Torpedo tubes 5 18". Main armour 6" to 4" belt to 7" to 6" bulkheads, 7" to 2" barbettes with 7" turrets, 10" conning tower, 2½" to 1" decks, 2½" magazines. Engines and speed Turbines; 41,000 h.p.; 25 knots. Remarks. All had their fore funnels raised before 1915.

CANOPUS Class battleships

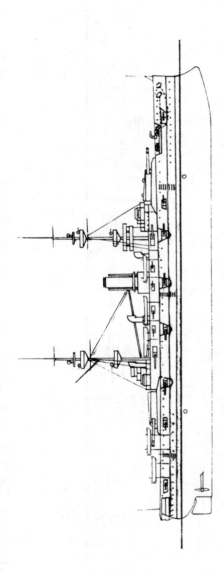

ALBION 1898, *CANOPUS* 1897, GLORY 1899, GOLIATH 1898, OCEAN 1898, VENGEANCE 1899
12,950 tons 390' × 74' × 25¾'. Guns 4 12", 12 6", 10 12-pdrs., 6 3-pdrs., 10 12-pdrs., 6 3-pdrs. Torpedo tubes 4 18" *(submerged).* Main armour *(Steel, belt and barbette Krupp)* 6" *belt,* 10" *to 6" forward bulkhead,* 12" *to 6" aft bulkhead,* 12" *to 6" barbettes with 8" shields,* 2" *to 1" decks,* 12" *conning towers.* Engines and speed *Triple expansion;* 13,500 *h.p.;* 18¼ *knots.* Remarks *Built shallow draught to go through the Suez Canal.*

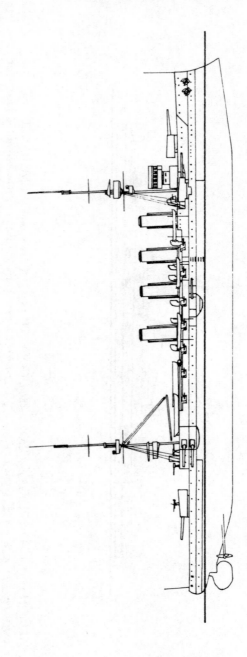

DEVONSHIRE Class cruisers

ANTRIM 1903, ARGYLL 1904, CARNARVON 1903, DEVONSHIRE 1904, HAMPSHIRE 1903, ROXBURGH 1904

10,850 tons 450′ × 68′ × 25′. Guns 4 7·5″, 6 6″, 2 12-pdrs, 20 3-pdrs. Torpedo tubes 2 18″ (submerged). Main armour 6″ to 2″ belt, 6″ bulkheads, 6″ barbettes with 5″ turrets, 6″ turrets, 6″ turrets, 12″ conning tower, 2″ deck. Engines and speed Triple expansion; 21,000 b.p.; 22¼ knots.

MONMOUTH Class cruisers

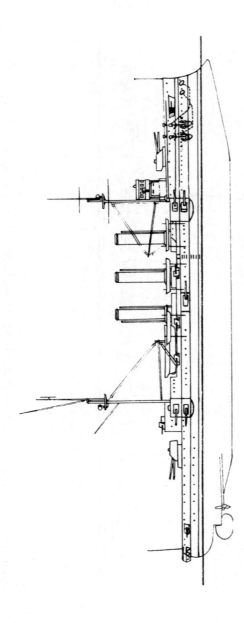

BEDFORD 1901, BERWICK 1902, *CORNWALL* 1902, CUMBERLAND 1902, DONEGAL 1902, ESSEX 1901, *KENT* 1901, LANCASTER 1902, MONMOUTH 1901, SUFFOLK 1903 *9,800 tons* 448' (*o/a*) × 66' × 24½'. Guns 14 6", 9 12-*pdrs*, 3 3-*pdrs*. Torpedo tubes 2 18" (*submerged*). Main armour 4" to 2" belt, 5" *bulkheads*, 5" *barbettes and turrets*, 4" *casemates*, 10" *conning tower*, 2" *deck*. Engines and speed *Triple expansion*; 22,000 *b.p.*; 23 *knots*.

BRISTOL Class light-cruisers

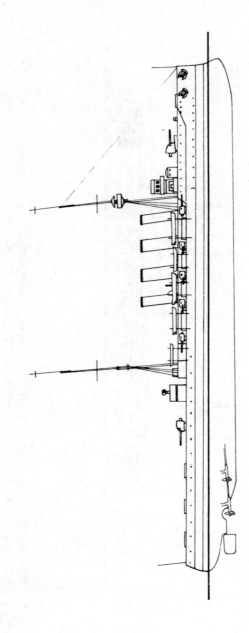

BRISTOL 1910, *GLASGOW*, GLOUCESTER, LIVERPOOL, NEWCASTLE, all 1909 4,800 *tons* 453' (*o/a*) × 47' × 15¼'. Guns 2 6", 10 4", 4 3-*pdrs.* (*saluting*). Torpedo tubes 2 18" (*submerged*). Main armour 6" *conning tower*, 4" *torpedo tubes*, 3" *to* ¾" *deck*. Engines and speed *Turbines*; 22,000 *b.p.*; 25 *knots*. Remarks Bristol *had twin screws, the others four.*

BIBLIOGRAPHY

Bennett, Geoffrey, *Coronel and the Falklands*, Pan, London, 1967, reprinted 1982.

Churchill, Winston, *The World Crisis 1911–1918*, Cassell, London, 1932.

Goebel, Julius, *The Struggle for the Falkland Islands*, Yale, 1982.

Hirst, Lloyd, *Coronel and After*, Peter Davies, London, 1934.

Irving, John, *Coronel and the Falklands*, A. M. Philpot, 1927.

Middlemas, Keith, *Command the Far Seas*, Hutchinson, London, 1961.

Millington-Drake, Eugen, *The Drama of Graf Spee and the Battle of the Plate*, Peter Davies, London, 1964.

Pitt, Barrie, *Coronel and Falkland*, Cassell, London, 1960.

Stirling, Bishop, *The Falkland Islands and Tierra del Fuego*, 1969.

Strange, Ian J., *The Falkland Islands*, David & Charles, Newton Abbott, 1981

BIOGRAPHICAL NOTE

Surgeon Captain T. B. Dixon, C.B.E., M.R.C.S., L.R.C.P., K.H.P., V.D., R.N.V.R. Thomas Benjamin Dixon was born in China in 1886, the son of Mr and Mrs Herbert Dixon, missionaries in Tiensin. His parents were killed in the Boxer rebellion while he was still a boy. Brought up by guardians in England and educated at Blackheath Dixon qualified in medicine at University College Hospital, London. He was an enthusiastic mountaineer.

He married Miss B. N. Lane of Clifton and, except for the war years, they lived in Bristol where he practised for nearly 40 years.

During both wars he served in the Navy, and between the wars continued his work with the R.N.V.R. in Bristol as P.M.O. of the Severn Division and later as Surgeon Captain. He was appointed Honorary Physician to H.M. King George VI, and was awarded the C.B.E. in 1945 for his service during World War 2.

He retired to live in Bantham, South Devon, where he continued to lead an active life until his death in 1960, aged 73.

INDEX

  i. **General**
  ii. **People**
  iii. **Places**
  iv. **Ships: British, German and other**
  v. **Wildlife**

i. GENERAL
Action Stations 22, 26, 28, 29, 53, 58

Bad weather 1–2, 24, 26, 32, 36, 49, 52, 56, 66, 76
Botany 14, 34, 35, 45, 48, 49, 51, 57, 67, 72

Coaling 5, 6, 10, 14, 16–18, 20, 32, 34, 37, 40, 42, 43, 46, 48, 52, 57, 65, 66, 67, 71, 72, 75
Chilean navy 61
Coronel (news of battle) 18, 21, 22

Dancing 11, 12, 35, 43, 56, 68, 71
Dress 4, 13, 14, 15, 24, 27, 33, 38, 42, 75
Doldrums 71

Entertainments 11, 21, 25, 35, 36, 40, 43, 49, 65, 68, 70–71, 74

Fleet, the 23
Fishing 11, 12, 20, 22, 23, 37, 39, 41, 44, 46, 48, 54–55, 56, 64, 65, 67, 71

'General quarters' 2, 6, 19–20, 46
Glaciers 32, 33, 50, 52, 53

Kent Kronikal 20, 23, 24, 34, 35, 37, 47

Lyddite 29, 30, 39

Mail censoring 4, 7, 16, 21, 35
Mails 18, 20, 21, 22, 23, 36, 37, 38, 44, 45, 47, 49, 66
Medical cases 6, 8, 9, 13, 21, 29, 30, 31, 32, 46, 59, 60, 61, 67
Mexican navy 74
Mountains 3, 4–5, 7–8, 9, 10, 13, 32, 33, 34, 37, 38, 40, 41, 45, 47–48, 52, 53, 64, 72, 75

Natives 14, 41, 48, 51, 60, 69
Newspapers 9, 12, 20, 21, 36, 42, 45, 47, 61, 66

Peruvian navy 42
Provisions 5, 8, 9, 12, 18, 23, 36, 37, 38, 41, 43, 45, 49, 69, 70

S.E. trades, wind 15
Sports 2, 10, 15, 20, 40, 44, 48, 49, 57, 70, 71

Target practice 3, 4, 6, 11, 19, 21, 22, 24, 38, 39, 44, 47, 54
Torpedoes 21, 22, 47, 51, 59, 76
Trips ashore 5, 9, 14, 35, 42, 46, 47, 51, 57, 60, 61, 67

Wireless messages 9, 11, 14, 18, 19, 24, 25, 33, 36, 37, 43, 50, 53
Wullywahs 53

ii. PEOPLE
Allen, John D., captain, *Kent* 4, 5, 6, 7, 10, 11, 12, 13, 14, 15, 25, 27, 34, 44, 65, 70
Andrews, Sydney G., paymaster, *Kent* 1, 3,

8, 10, 20, 30, 35
Ashton, Mrs 43, 68
Assenheimer, *Orama* 63, 71

Bilben, sick bay steward, *Kent* 29, 30, 39
Bedford, Arthur E. F., commander, *Kent*
    9, 11, 14, 25, 29, 33, 38, 69, 72
Burn, Ronald E. B., temporary surgeon,
    Kent 2, 7, 9, 11, 13, 16, 20, 29, 35, 42,
    43, 59, 61, 67, 71
Burridge, Robert L., midshipman, *Kent* 51

Cargill 38
Carver, lieutenant R.N.R., *Orama* 63
Clark 49

Danckwerts, Victor H., gunnery
    lieutenant, *Kent* 4, 5, 11, 40, 77
Dixon, David Falkland 66, 68, 77
Dixon, Norah 13, 20, 62, 70
Dunn, Harold T., lieutenant R.N.R., *Kent*
    31, 35

Foreman, Victor O., eng. lieutenant, *Kent*
    29, 54

Garner, Mr & Mrs 57
Gilmour, fleet surgeon 60, 61

Hadden, fleet surgeon, *Victorian* 8
Hamilton 14
Hammond, Mr & Mrs 67
Harvey, James R., lieutenant commander
    (N), *Kent* 67
Heal, *Orama* 63, 68
Healey, captain, *Orotara* 61, 63, 64
Hiley, Mr & Mrs 9
Howard, Frederick C., lieutenant R.N.R.,
    Kent 43, 65

Illiewicz, fleet surgeon, *Marmora* 13

Jenkins, gunlayer, *Kent* 40
Johnson 42, 70, 71
Johnson, captain, *Eggesford* 69
Jones, William G. B., lieutenant R.N.R.,
    Kent 35, 40, 71

Kelly, royal marine, *Kent* 30
Kent, Rev. N. B., padre, *Kent* 2, 3, 4, 10,
    14, 35, 49, 72

Laing, Robert W. J., captain of royal
    marines, *Kent* 1, 14, 35, 36, 65, 71

Lane, Grace 66
Liley, George C. B., midshipman R.N.R.,
    Kent 40
Lloyd, temporary surgeon, *Victorian* 8
Loveday 49
Luce, John, captain, *Glasgow* 59
Lüdecke, captain, *Dresden* 59, 60

Marshall, James, lieutenant R.N.R., *Kent*
    29
Mayes, Charles, sergeant R.M.L.I., *Kent*
    30
MacIver 42, 68
Munnich, Dr 61

Pickthorn, Edward B., (P.M.O.) fleet
    surgeon, *Kent* 1, 2, 3, 4, 7, 14, 16, 17,
    20, 23, 35, 42, 46, 54, 55, 61, 67

Rayner, Alfred E. E., lieutenant
    commander, *Kent* 46
Redhead, Charles M., lieutenant
    commander, *Kent* 2, 8, 9, 11, 22, 41, 43,
    47, 49, 65

Salter, private R.M.L.I., *Kent* 46
Seagrave, captain, *Orama* 63, 72
Scowcroft, surgeon, *Orama* 63
Shackleton, Sir Ernest 77
Skinner, Osborne W., eng. lieutenant,
    Kent 46
Stewart, William G., assistant paymaster
    R.N.R., *Kent* 11, 25
Stockman, Belgian vice consul, Lima 70
Stoddart, A. P., rear admiral, *Defence* 20,
    24
Sturdee, Sir Doveton, admiral of the fleet
    23, 24, 26

Taylor, consul, Cape Verde 5
Tilling, Walter R., lieutenant R.N.R., *Kent*
    44
Trench, surgeon, *Carnarvon* 21

Welham, senior temp. surgeon, *Orama* 63
Wharton, Eric L., lieutenant commander
    (T), *Kent* 22, 33, 37, 38, 47, 49, 51, 53, 56,
    67, 72
Williams, commander, *Carnarvon* 21
Wingfield, Mrs 43, 68
Wizard, fleet surgeon 60
Woodhouse, Harry 67

iii. PLACES

Abrolhos Rocks 15, 16, 17, 19, 20, 22, 23, 24, 41
Alert Bay 50
Ancon Bay 40, 41
Anconcagua 37
Antofagasta 43, 44, 45

Bahia 22
Barbara Channel 52, 53, 54
Bay of Biscay 1
Beagle Channel 49
Bedford Bay 53
Bissagos Islands 9
Blanco-Encalada 45
Brodrip Bay 53

Callao 40, 42, 43, 66, 67, 68
Canary Islands 7
Cape Horn 26
Cape Mendocino 76
Cape Rapier 34
Chonos Islands 34
Cockburn Channel 53
Cocos Islands 71, 72
Coquimbo 38, 46
Concepcion 36
Coronel 36, 49, 54, 56, 57
Cumberland Bay 58

Dakar 10, 11, 12, 77
Darwin Channel 34

Elizabeth Island 32
Equator 15, 71
Esquimalt 71, 72, 75, 77

Galapagos Islands 68, 69, 72
Gonzales Channel 52

Icy Sound 52, 53
Independencia Bay 40
Iquique 43, 44

Juan Fernandez 54, 57, 58–60, 63

Kirk Narrows 50

Las Palmas 9
La Serena 38
Last Hope Inlet 49, 50, 54
Lima 41, 42, 43, 66, 67–68, 70–71

Madeira 3, 6

Magdalen Channel 52
MasAfuera 58, 60, 63, 64
Mazatlan 77
Mexico 44, 75, 76, 77
Mollendo 43, 66
Monte Video 18, 24
Mount Sarmiento 52, 53
Mount Wharton 33

Paita 68, 69, 73
Panama 42
Patagonia 32
Plymouth 77
Portsmouth 4
Port Stanley 26, 31, 77
Port Tamar 50
Punta Arenas 32, 49, 51, 52

Rio de Janeiro 22, 23

San Bartolome 74, 75
San Francisco 76
San Nicholas Bay 40, 41, 42, 67, 68
Santa Cruz 8
Santa Maria Island 49, 56
Sechura Bay 69, 71
Shag Narrows 54
Sholl Bay 52
Sierra Leone 12, 13, 14, 16
Simonstown 77
Smyth's Sound 41, 49, 50, 51
Socorro Island 73, 74
South Georgia 77
St Felix (Islands) 39
St Helena 23
St Vincent 1, 4–5, 10
Straits of Magellan 26, 32–33, 34, 42, 50, 52

Tamar Island 33
Tenerife 7, 8, 9
Three Finger Island 47
Tierra del Fuego 32, 52
Tongoy Bay 37
Trinidad Inlet 50

ValleNar Roads 34, 36, 47, 51
Valparaiso 19, 36, 38, 44, 45, 46, 49, 54, 61, 66
Vancouver 76

iv. BRITISH SHIPS
Amazon, S.S., R.M.S.P. 18

Braunton (collier) 46
Bristol, H.M.S. 22, 23, 27, 34, 36, 39, 49, 50, 51, 52, 53, 54, 56

Cairncross (collier) 52
Canopus, H.M.S. 21, 26
Carmania (merchant-cruiser) 8
Carnarvon, H.M.S. 6, 20, 22, 23, 24, 27
Celtic (liner) 44, 45, 46, 47
Cornwall, H.M.S. 20, 23, 27, 28, 29
Crown of Bangor, S.S. 23

Defence, H.M.S. 6, 19, 20, 23

Edinburgh Castle, H.M.S. 18, 20, 21
Eggesford (collier) 69
Empress of Britain (merchant-cruiser) 5
Europa, H.M.S. 1
Formidable, H.M.S. 37

Gillingham, H.M.S. 51
Glasgow, H.M.S. 22, 23, 27, 28, 34, 36, 49, 50, 51, 52, 53, 54, 56, 58, 59
Good Hope, H.M.S. 18, 19, 20

Hawke, H.M.S. 5
Highflyer, H.M.S. 11, 12

Inflexible, H.M.S. 20, 23, 27, 28
Invicta (dinghy) 70
Invincible, H.M.S. 20, 23, 27, 28

Macedonia, H.M.S. 25, 27, 66
Marmora 7, 13, 15
Monmouth, H.M.S. 18, 19, 20

Newcastle, H.M.S. 43, 44, 72

Orama, H.M.S. 7, 12, 20, 23, 33, 34, 36, 37, 38, 40, 41, 43, 44, 45, 46, 47, 49, 52, 54, 58, 59, 60, 61, 63–65, 66, 67, 68, 69, 71, 72
Orissa (liner) 41
Orita (liner) 36, 66, 68
Orotava (liner) 61
Ortega (liner) 20, 41
Otranto, H.M.S. 20, 21

Pensilva (collier) 34, 36, 37
Peru, S.S. 44, 45

Rainbow, H.M.S. 75

Thistleton (collier) 16

Trevanion (collier) 32, 36, 43

Vasari, S.S. 9
Vectis, S.S. 8
Victorian, H.M.S. 8
Vindictive, H.M.S. 7

GERMAN AND OTHER SHIPS
Ancobra (steamer) 12
Ariadne-Irene, S.S. N.Z.S.Co. 12

Blucher 43

Dresden (German warship) 27, 28, 29, 31, 33, 41, 49, 50, 51, 52, 53, 54, 55–56, 58–61

Espagne (French liner) 10

Gneisenau (German warship) 18, 19, 26, 27, 28
Gotha (German collier) 54, 56

Kaiser Wilhelm der Grosse (German warship) 11, 12
Karlsruhe (German warship) 6, 7, 9, 11, 24
Kronprinz Wilhelm (German warship) 24

Leipzig (German warship) 28–29

Nürnberg (German warship) 27, 28, 29, 30–31

Oetz (Danish) 2
Osama (Japanese) 69, 75

Prinz Eitel Friedrich (German warship) 38, 43, 49

Scharnhorst (German warship) 18, 28
Shitushi (Japanese repair ship) 75

v. WILDLIFE
Albacore 68
Albatross 25, 34, 54, 76

Bonita 41
Bream 23, 39, 64

Cavalli 64, 65
Coral fish 73
Crab 39

Dogfish 68
Donkey, wild 72

Eels 41, 65, 74

Flying fish 12

Garfish 23
Goat, wild 64
Guanaco 32

Halibut 68
Herring hake 56

Lizard 72
Lobster 65, 66

'Mother Carey's Chickens' 2
Mullet 39, 65, 68

Nautilus 76

Octopus 37, 48

Pelican 67
Pig, ship's 48, 76
Pig, wild 73
Plaice 68
Porpoise 12

Rock cod 39, 46, 65, 73, 74, 76

Seal 48, 67
Sealion 40, 72
Seasnake 65
Shag 54, 67
Shark 11, 22, 54–55, 65, 72, 74
Skate 68
Snake 72
Sheep, wild 73, 74
Sooty tern 39

Turtle 73, 75, 76

Vicuna 48, 51, 71

Whale 25, 37, 73

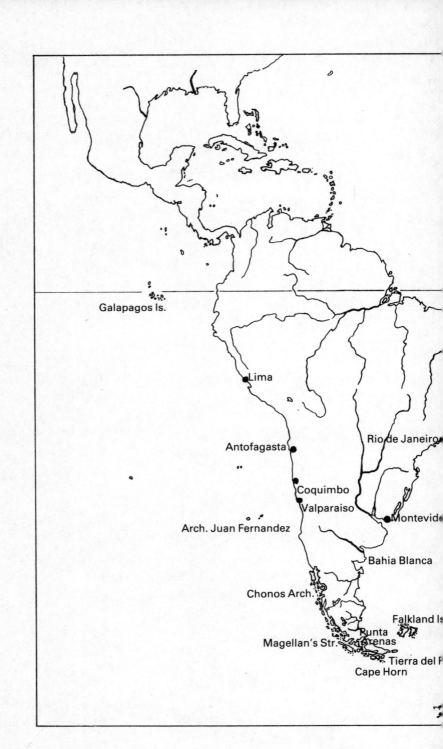